TRUTHS
MOST WORTH
KNOWING

TRUTHS
MOST WORTH
KNOWING

An Apostle's Witness

BOYD K. PACKER

**DESERET
BOOK**

SALT LAKE CITY, UTAH

The painting on pages 96–97 was painted by Boyd K. Packer in 1990. Its title, *The Presidency*, was inspired by comments President Packer heard as a boy from older people, who referred to the three solid mountains of Willard Peaks by that name.

© 2015 Boyd K. Packer

Library of Congress Cataloging-in-Publication Data

(CIP data on file)
ISBN 978-1-62972-096-8

Printed in China
RR Donnelley, Shenzhen, China

10 9 8 7 6 5 4 3 2 1

Contents

CONTENTS

Introduction

All knowledge is not necessarily of equal value. The value of knowledge is determined by how it can be used. Some things can be interesting or entertaining. Other knowledge can be hurtful or even destructive and is not worth knowing, remembering, or sharing. Just because something is true does not make it valuable or right.

Some knowledge is beyond just being valuable. These truths can be crucial to happiness as well as to exaltation. Acting on these principles and truths is the only way to qualify for exaltation. An individual's testimony and knowledge of the existence of Jesus Christ and His Atonement and great plan of happiness are of the greatest value to mankind.

From my service as a General Authority for more than fifty years, I have gathered together a collection of truths worth knowing. The most important truth is, of course, my witness of Jesus Christ. In these pages, to present these truths, I have shared stories and experiences that teach the gospel in a way that I hope will make the principles of happiness easy to understand and remember.

Part One

FAITH IN THE LORD JESUS CHRIST AND HIS ATONEMENT

CHAPTER 1

The Witness

Times of war or uncertainty have a way of sharpening our focus on things that really matter.

World War II was a time of great spiritual turmoil for me. I had left my home in Brigham City, Utah, with only embers of a testimony, and I felt the need for something more. Virtually our whole senior class in a matter of weeks was on its way to the war zone. While stationed on the island of Ie Shima, just north of Okinawa, Japan, I struggled with doubt and uncertainty. I wanted a personal testimony of the gospel. I wanted to *know!*

During one sleepless night, I left my tent and entered a bunker that had been formed by lining up fifty-gallon fuel drums filled with sand and placed one on top of the other to

_____

From a talk given at general conference, April 2014.

3

form an enclosure. There was no roof, and so I crawled in, looked up at the star-filled sky, and knelt to pray.

Almost midsentence it happened. I could not describe to you what happened if I were determined to do so. It is beyond my power of expression, but it is as clear today as it was that night more than sixty-five years ago. I knew it to be a very private, very individual manifestation. At last I knew for myself. I *knew* for a certainty, for it had been given to me. After some time, I crawled from that bunker and walked, or floated, back to my bed. I spent the rest of the night in a feeling of joy and awe.

Far from thinking I was someone special, I thought that if such a thing came to me, that it could come to anyone. I still believe that. In the years that have followed, I have come to understand that such an experience is at once a light to follow and a burden to carry.

I wish to share with you those truths that are the most worth knowing, the things that I have learned and experienced in nearly ninety years of life and over fifty years as a General Authority. Much of what I have come to know falls into the category of things that cannot be taught but can be learned.

Like most things of great worth, knowledge that is of eternal value comes only through personal prayer and pondering. These, joined with fasting and scripture study, will invite impressions and revelations and the whisperings of the Holy Spirit. This provides us with instruction from on high as we learn precept upon precept.

The revelations promise that "whatever principle of intelligence we attain unto in this life, it will rise with us in the resurrection" and that "knowledge and intelligence [are gained] through . . . diligence and obedience" (D&C 130:18–19).

One eternal truth that I have come to know is that God lives. He is our Father. We are His children. "We believe in God, the Eternal Father, and in His Son, Jesus Christ, and in the Holy Ghost" (Articles of Faith 1:1).

Of all the other titles that He could have used, He chose to be called "Father." The Savior commanded, "After this manner therefore pray ye: Our Father who art in heaven" (3 Nephi 13:9; see also Matthew 6:9). His use of the name "Father" is a lesson for all as we come to understand what it is that matters most in this life.

Parenthood is a sacred privilege, and, depending upon faithfulness, it can be an eternal blessing. The ultimate end of all activity in the Church is that a man and his wife and their children can be happy at home.

Those who do not marry or those who cannot have children are not excluded from the eternal blessings that they seek but that, for now, remain beyond their reach. We do not always know how or when blessings will present themselves, but the promise of eternal increase will not be denied any faithful individual who makes and keeps sacred covenants.

Your secret yearnings and tearful pleadings will touch the heart of both the Father and the Son. You will be given a personal assurance from Them that your life will be full and that no blessing that is essential will be lost to you.

As a servant of the Lord, acting in the office to which I have been ordained, I give those in such circumstances a promise that there will be nothing essential to your salvation and exaltation that shall not in due time rest upon you. Arms now empty will be filled, and hearts now hurting from broken dreams and yearning will be healed.

Another truth I have come to know is that the Holy Ghost is real. He is the third member of the Godhead. His mission is to testify of truth and righteousness. He manifests Himself in many ways, including feelings of peace and reassurance. He can also bring comfort, guidance, and correction when needed. The companionship of the Holy Ghost is maintained throughout our lives by righteous living.

The gift of the Holy Ghost is conferred through an ordinance of the gospel. One with authority lays his hands on the head of a new member of the Church and says words such as these: "Receive the Holy Ghost."

This ordinance alone does not change us in a noticeable way, but if we listen and follow the promptings, we will receive the blessing of the Holy Ghost. Each son or daughter of our Heavenly Father can come to know the reality of Moroni's promise: "By the power of the Holy Ghost ye may know the *truth* of all things" (Moroni 10:5; emphasis added).

A supernal truth that I have gained in my life is my witness of the Lord Jesus Christ.

Foremost and underpinning all that we do, anchored throughout the revelations, is the Lord's name, which is the authority by which we act in the Church. Every prayer offered, even by little children, ends in the name of Jesus Christ. Every blessing, every ordinance, every ordination, every official act is done in the name of Jesus Christ. It is His Church, and it

KNOWLEDGE

that is of

ETERNAL VALUE

comes only

through

PERSONAL PRAYER

and

PONDERING.

is named for Him—The Church of Jesus Christ of Latter-day Saints (see D&C 115:4).

There is that great incident in the Book of Mormon where the Nephites "were praying unto the Father in [the Lord's] name." The Lord appeared and asked:

"What will ye that I shall give unto you?

"And they said unto him: Lord, we will that thou wouldst tell us the name whereby we shall call this church; for there are disputations among the people concerning this matter.

"And the Lord said unto them: Verily, verily, I say unto you, why is it that the people should murmur and dispute because of this thing?

"Have they not read the scriptures, which say ye must take upon you the name of Christ, which is my name? For by this name shall ye be called at the last day;

"And whoso taketh upon him my name, and endureth to the end, the same shall be saved. . . .

"Therefore, whatsoever ye shall do, ye shall do it in my name; therefore ye shall call the church in my name; and ye shall call upon the Father in my name that he will bless the church for my sake" (3 Nephi 27:2–7).

It is His name, Jesus Christ, "for there is none other name under heaven given among men, whereby we must be saved" (Acts 4:12).

In the Church we know who He is: Jesus Christ, the Son of God. He is the Only Begotten of the Father. He is He who was slain and He who liveth again. He is our Advocate with the Father. "Remember that it is upon the rock of our Redeemer, who is Christ, the Son of God, that [we] must build

[our] foundation" (Helaman 5:12). He is the anchor that holds us and protects us and our families through the storms of life.

Each Sunday across the world where congregations gather of any nationality or tongue, the sacrament is blessed with the same words. We take upon ourselves the name of Christ and always remember Him. That is imprinted upon us.

Each of us must come to our own personal testimony of the Lord Jesus Christ. We then share that testimony with our family and others.

In all of this, let us remember that there is an adversary who personally seeks to disrupt the work of the Lord. We must choose whom to follow. Our protection is as simple as deciding individually to follow the Savior, making certain that we faithfully will remain on His side.

In the New Testament, John records that there were some who were unable to commit to the Savior and His teachings, and "from that time many of his disciples went back, and walked no more with him.

"Then said Jesus unto the twelve, Will ye also go away?

"Then Simon Peter answered him, Lord, to whom shall we go? thou hast the words of eternal life.

"And we believe and are sure that thou art that Christ, the Son of the living God" (John 6:66–69).

Peter had gained that which can be learned by each follower of the Savior. To be faithfully devoted to Jesus Christ, we accept Him as our Redeemer and do all within our power to live His teachings.

After all the years that I have lived and taught and served, after the millions of miles I have traveled around the world, with all that I have experienced, there is one great truth that I would share. That is my witness of the Savior Jesus Christ.

Joseph Smith and Sidney Rigdon recorded the following after a sacred experience:

"And now, after the many testimonies which have been given of him, this is the testimony, last of all, which we give of him: That he lives!

"For we saw him" (D&C 76:22–23).

Their words are my words.

I believe and *I* am sure that Jesus is the Christ, the Son of God, and that He lives. He is the Only Begotten of the Father, and "by him, and through him, and of him, the worlds are and were created, and the inhabitants thereof are begotten sons and daughters unto God" (D&C 76:24).

I bear my witness that the Savior lives. I *know* the Lord. I am His witness. I know of His great sacrifice and eternal love for all of Heavenly Father's children. I bear my special witness in all humility but with absolute certainty.

CHAPTER 2

Who Is Jesus Christ?

Meeting with the Twelve at Caesarea Philippi, Jesus asked, "Whom say ye that I am?" Simon Peter, the chief Apostle, answered, "Thou art the Christ, the Son of the living God" (Matthew 16:15–16). Peter later testified that Jesus "was foreordained before the foundation of the world" (1 Peter 1:20). He was "in the beginning with the Father, and [is] the Firstborn" (D&C 93:21).

When the Father's plan—the plan of salvation and happiness (see Alma 34:9)—was presented (see Alma 42:5, 8), one was required to atone to provide redemption and mercy to all those who accepted the plan (see Alma 34:16; 39:18; 42:15). The Father asked, "Whom shall I send?" He who was to be known as Jesus freely and willingly chose to answer, "Here am I,

Adapted from an article in Ensign, *March 2008, 12–19.*

send me" (Abraham 3:27). "Father, thy will be done, and the glory be thine forever" (Moses 4:2).

In preparation, the earth was created: "By the Son I created [the earth], which is mine Only Begotten," declared the Father (Moses 1:33; see also Ephesians 3:9; Helaman 14:12; Moses 2:1).

Titles of Jesus Christ

He was known as Jehovah by the Old Testament prophets (see Abraham 1:16; Exodus 6:3). The prophets were shown of His coming: "Behold the Lamb of God, yea, even the Son of the Eternal Father!" (1 Nephi 11:21; see also John 1:14). His mother was told, "Call his name Jesus. . . . He shall be . . . called the Son of the Highest" (Luke 1:31–32).

Many titles and names are descriptive of His divine mission and ministry. He Himself taught: "I am the light and the life of the world. I am Alpha and Omega, the beginning and the end" (3 Nephi 9:18). "I am . . . your advocate with the Father" (D&C 29:5; see also D&C 110:14). "I am the good shepherd" (John 10:11). "I am Messiah, the King of Zion, the Rock of Heaven" (Moses 7:53). "I am the bread of life: he that cometh to me shall never hunger . . . [or] thirst" (John 6:35). "I am the true vine, and my Father is the husbandman" (John 15:1). "I am the resurrection, and the life" (John 11:25). "I am . . . the bright and morning star" (Revelation 22:16), "Jesus Christ, your Redeemer, the Great I Am" (D&C 29:1).

He is the Mediator (see 1 Timothy 2:5), the Savior (see Luke 2:11), the Redeemer (see D&C 18:47), the Head of the Church (see Ephesians 5:23), its Chief Cornerstone (see Ephesians 2:20). At the last day, "God shall judge . . . men by Jesus Christ according to [the] gospel" (Romans 2:16; see also Mormon 3:20).

"God so loved the world, that he gave his only begotten Son" (John 3:16); "wherefore, redemption cometh in and through the Holy Messiah; for he is full of grace and truth" (2 Nephi 2:6).

The Prophet Joseph Smith was often asked, "What are the fundamental principles of your religion?"

His answer: "The fundamental principles of our religion are the testimony of the Apostles and Prophets, concerning Jesus Christ, that He died, was buried, and rose again the third day, and ascended into heaven; and all other things which pertain to our religion are only appendages to it" (*Teachings of Presidents of the Church: Joseph Smith* [2007], 49).

Humility of Jesus Christ

At the time of His arrest before His Crucifixion, the Lord had come from Gethsemane. At the moment of betrayal, Peter drew his sword against Malchus, a servant of the high priest. Jesus said:

"Put up again thy sword into his place. . . .

"Thinkest thou that I cannot now pray to my Father, and he shall presently give me more than twelve legions of angels?" (Matthew 26:52–53).

During all of the taunting, abuse, scourging, and final torture of crucifixion, the Lord remained silent and submissive—

except, that is, for one moment of intense drama that reveals the very essence of Christian doctrine. That moment came during the trial. Pilate, now afraid, said to Jesus: "Speakest thou not unto me? knowest thou not that I have power to crucify thee, and have power to release thee?" (John 19:10).

One can only imagine the quiet majesty when the Lord spoke: "Thou couldest have no power at all against me, except it were given thee from above" (John 19:11). What happened thereafter did not come because Pilate had power to impose it but because the Lord had the will to accept it.

"I lay down my life," the Lord said, "that I might take it again.

"No man taketh it from me, but I lay it down of myself. I have power to lay it down, and I have power to take it again" (John 10:17–18).

Atonement of Jesus Christ

Before the Crucifixion and afterward, many have willingly given their lives in selfless acts of heroism. But none faced what Christ endured. Upon Him was the burden of all human transgression, all human guilt. And hanging in the balance was the Atonement. Through His willing act, mercy and justice could be reconciled, eternal law sustained, and that mediation achieved without which mortal men and women could not be redeemed.

He by choice accepted the penalty in behalf of all mankind for the sum total of all wickedness and depravity; for brutality, immorality, perversion, and corruption; for addiction; for the killings and torture and terror—for all of it that ever had been or all that ever would be enacted upon this earth. In so choosing He faced the awesome power of the evil one, who was not confined to flesh nor subject to mortal pain. That was Gethsemane!

How the Atonement was wrought we do not know. No mortal watched as evil turned away and hid in shame before the Light of that pure being. All wickedness could not quench that Light. When what was done was done, the ransom had been paid. Both death and hell forsook their claim on all who would repent. Men at last were free. Then every soul who ever lived could choose to touch that Light and be redeemed.

By this infinite sacrifice, "through [this] Atonement of Christ, all mankind may be saved, by obedience to the laws and ordinances of the Gospel" (Articles of Faith 1:3).

"Atonement" in Scripture

The English word *atonement* is really three words: *at-one-ment,* which means to set at one; one with God; to reconcile, to conciliate, to expiate.

But did you know that the word *atonement* appears only once in the English New Testament? Only once! I quote from Paul's letter to the Romans:

"Christ died for us.

" . . . We were reconciled to God by the death of his Son, much more, being reconciled, we shall be saved by his life.

"And not only so, but we also joy in God through our Lord

Jesus Christ, by whom we have now received the *atonement*" (Romans 5:8, 10–11; emphasis added).

Only that once does the word *atonement* appear in the English New Testament. *Atonement,* of all words! It was not an unknown word, for it had been used much in the Old Testament in connection with the law of Moses, but once only in the New Testament. I find that to be remarkable.

I know of only one explanation. For that we turn to the Book of Mormon. Nephi testified that the Bible once "contained the fulness of the gospel of the Lord, of whom the twelve apostles bear record" and that "after [the words] go forth by the hand of the twelve apostles of the Lamb, from the Jews unto the Gentiles, thou seest the formation of that great and abominable church, which is most abominable above all other churches; for behold, they have taken away from the gospel of the Lamb many parts which are plain and most precious; and also many covenants of the Lord have they taken away" (1 Nephi 13:24, 26).

Jacob defined the great and abominable church in these words: "Wherefore, he that fighteth against Zion, both Jew and Gentile, both bond and free, both male and female, shall perish; for they are they who are the whore of all the earth; for they who are not for me are against me, saith our God" (2 Nephi 10:16).

Nephi also said, "Because of the many plain and precious things which have been taken out of the book, . . . an exceedingly great many do stumble, yea, insomuch that Satan hath great power over them" (1 Nephi 13:29). He then prophesied

If punishment is

the price repentance asks,

IT COMES AT BARGAIN PRICE.

Consequences,

EVEN PAINFUL ONES,

PROTECT US.

that the precious things would be restored (see 1 Nephi 13:34–35).

And they were restored. In the Book of Mormon the word *atone* in form and tense appears thirty-nine times. I quote but one verse from Alma: "And now, the plan of mercy could not be brought about except an *atonement* should be made; therefore God himself *atoneth* for the sins of the world, to bring about the plan of mercy, to appease the demands of justice, that God might be a perfect, just God, and a merciful God also" (Alma 42:15; emphasis added).

Atonement: used only once in the New Testament but thirty-nine times in the Book of Mormon. What better witness that the Book of Mormon is indeed another testament of Jesus Christ?

And that is not all. The words *atone, atoneth,* and *atonement* appear in the Doctrine and Covenants five times and in the Pearl of Great Price twice. Forty-six references of transcendent importance. And that is not all! Hundreds of other verses help to explain the Atonement.

Agency

The cost of the Atonement was borne by the Lord without compulsion, for agency is a sovereign principle. According to the plan, agency must be honored. It was so from the beginning, from Eden.

"The Lord said unto Enoch: Behold these thy brethren; they are the workmanship of mine own hands, and I gave unto them their knowledge, in the day I created them; and in the Garden of Eden, gave I unto man his agency" (Moses 7:32).

Whatever else happened in Eden, in his supreme moment of testing, Adam made a choice. After the Lord commanded Adam and Eve to multiply and replenish the earth and commanded them not to partake of the tree of knowledge of good and evil, He said, "Nevertheless, thou mayest choose for thyself, for it is given unto thee; but, remember that I forbid it, for in the day thou eatest thereof thou shalt surely die" (Moses 3:17).

There was too much at issue to introduce man into mortality by force. That would contravene the very law essential to the plan. The plan provided that each spirit child of God would receive a mortal body and each would be tested. Adam saw that it must be so and made his choice. "Adam fell that men might be; and men are, that they might have joy" (2 Nephi 2:25).

Adam and Eve ventured forth to multiply and replenish the earth as they had been commanded to do. The creation of their bodies in the image of God, as a separate creation, was crucial to the plan. Their subsequent Fall was essential if the condition of mortality was to exist and the plan to proceed.

Necessity of the Atonement

Jacob described what would happen to our bodies and our spirits except "an infinite atonement" was made. "Our spirits," he said, "must have become like unto [the devil]." (See 2 Nephi 9:7–10.)

I seldom use the word *absolutely.* It seldom fits. I use it now—twice:

Because of the Fall, the Atonement was *absolutely* essential for resurrection to proceed and overcome mortal death.

The Atonement was *absolutely* essential for men and women to cleanse themselves from sin and overcome the second death, spiritual death, which is separation from our Father in Heaven, for the scriptures tell us at least eight times that no unclean thing may enter the presence of God (see 1 Nephi 10:21; 15:34; Alma 7:21; 11:37; 40:26; Helaman 8:25; 3 Nephi 27:19; Moses 6:57).

Those scriptural words, "Thou mayest choose for thyself, for it is given unto thee" (Moses 3:17), introduced Adam and Eve and their posterity to all the risks of mortality. In mortality men are free to choose, and each choice begets a consequence. The choice Adam made energized the law of justice, which required that the penalty for disobedience would be death.

But those words spoken at Christ's trial, "Thou couldest have no power at all against me, except it were given thee from above" (John 19:11), proved mercy was of equal rank. A redeemer was sent to pay the debt and set men free. That was the plan.

Alma's son Corianton thought it unfair that penalties must follow sin, that there need be punishment. In a profound lesson, Alma taught the plan of redemption to his son and so to us. Alma spoke of the Atonement and said, "Now, repentance could not come unto men except there were a punishment" (Alma 42:16).

If punishment is the price repentance asks, it comes at

bargain price. Consequences, even painful ones, protect us. So simple a thing as a child's cry of pain when his finger touches fire can teach us that. Except for the pain, the child might be consumed.

Blessings of Repentance

I readily confess that I would find no peace, neither happiness nor safety, in a world without repentance. I do not know what I should do if there were no way for me to erase my mistakes. The agony would be more than I could bear. It may be otherwise with you, but not with me.

The Atonement was made. Ever and always it offers amnesty from transgression and from death if we will but repent. Repentance is the escape clause in it all. Repentance is the key with which we can unlock the prison from inside. We hold that key within our hands, and agency is ours to use it.

How supernally precious freedom is; how consummately valuable is agency.

Lucifer in clever ways manipulates our choices, deceiving us about sin and consequences. He and his angels tempt us to be unworthy, even wicked. But he cannot—in all eternity he cannot, with all his power he cannot—completely destroy us, not without our own consent. Had agency come to man without the Atonement, it would have been a fatal gift.

Created in His Image

We are taught in Genesis, in Moses, in Abraham, in the Book of Mormon, and in the temple endowment that man's mortal body was made in the image of God in a separate creation. Had the Creation come in a different way, there could have been no Fall.

If men were merely animals, then logic favors freedom without accountability.

How well I know that among the learned are those who look down at animals and stones to find the origin of man. They do not look inside themselves to find the spirit there. They train themselves to measure things by time, by thousands and by millions, and say these animals called men all came by chance. And this they are free to do, for agency is theirs.

But agency is ours as well. We look up, and in the universe we see the handiwork of God and measure things by epochs, by aeons, by dispensations, by eternities. The many things we do not know, we take on faith.

But this we know! It was all planned "before the world was" (D&C 38:1; see also D&C 49:17; 76:13, 39; 93:7; Abraham 3:22–25). Events from the Creation to the final, winding-up scene are not based on *chance;* they are based on *choice!* It was planned that way.

This we know! This simple truth! Had there been no Creation and no Fall, there should have been no need for any Atonement, neither a Redeemer to mediate for us. Then Christ need not have been.

Symbols of the Atonement

At Gethsemane and Golgotha, the Savior's blood was shed. Centuries earlier the Passover had been introduced as a symbol and a type of things to come. It was an ordinance to be kept forever (see Exodus 12).

When the plague of death was decreed upon Egypt, each Israelite family was commanded to take a lamb—firstborn, male, without blemish. This paschal lamb was slain without breaking any bones, its blood to mark the doorway of the home. The Lord promised that the angel of death would *pass over* the homes so marked and not slay those inside. They were saved by the blood of the lamb.

After the Crucifixion of the Lord, the law of sacrifice required no more shedding of blood. For that was done, as Paul taught the Hebrews, "once for all . . . one sacrifice for sins for ever" (Hebrews 10:10, 12). The sacrifice thenceforth was to be a broken heart and a contrite spirit—repentance.

And the Passover would be commemorated forever as the sacrament, in which we renew our covenant of baptism and partake in remembrance of the body of the Lamb of God and of His blood, which was shed for us.

It is no small thing that this symbol reappears in the Word of Wisdom. Beyond the promise that Saints in this generation who obey will receive health and great treasures of knowledge is this: "I, the Lord, give unto them a promise, that the destroying angel shall pass by them, as the children of Israel, and not slay them" (D&C 89:21).

I cannot with composure tell you how I feel about the Atonement. It touches the deepest emotions of gratitude and obligation. My soul reaches after Him who wrought it—this Christ, our Savior, of whom I am a witness. I testify of Him.

He is our Lord, our Redeemer, our Advocate with the Father. He ransomed us with His blood.

Humbly I lay claim upon the Atonement of Christ. I find no shame in kneeling down in worship of our Father and His Son. For *agency* is mine, and this I *choose* to do!

CHAPTER 3

The Atonement

This chapter is directed to those among us who are suffering, burdened down with guilt and weakness and failure, sorrow, and despair.

In 1971, I was assigned to stake conferences in Western Samoa, including the organization of a new stake on Upolu island. After interviews we chartered a small plane to Savai'i island to hold a stake conference there. The plane landed on a grassy field at Faala and was to return the next afternoon to take us back to Upolu island.

The day we were to return from Savai'i, it was raining. Knowing the plane could not land on the wet field, we drove to the west end of the island, where there was a runway of sorts atop a coral break. We waited until dark, but no plane arrived. Finally, we learned by radio that there was a storm, and the

---

From a talk given at general conference, October 2012.

plane could not take off. We radioed back that we would come by boat. Someone was to meet us at Mulifanua.

As we pulled out of port on Savai'i, the captain of the forty-foot boat asked the mission president if he had a flashlight. Fortunately, he did and made a present of it to the captain. We made the thirteen-mile crossing to Upolu island on very rough seas. None of us realized that a ferocious tropical storm had hit the island, and we were heading straight into it.

We arrived in the harbor at Mulifanua. There was one narrow passage we were to go through along the reef. A light on the hill above the beach and a second lower light marked the narrow passage. When a boat was maneuvered so that the two lights were one above the other, the boat would be lined up properly to pass through the dangerous rocks that lined the passage.

But that night there was only one light. Two elders were waiting on the landing to meet us, but the crossing took much longer than usual. After watching for hours for signs of our boat, the elders tired and fell asleep, neglecting to turn on the second light, the lower light. As a result, the passage through the reef was not clear.

The captain maneuvered the boat as best he could toward the one upper light on shore while a crewman held the borrowed flashlight over the bow, searching for rocks ahead. We could hear the breakers crashing over the reef. When we were close enough to see them with the flashlight, the captain frantically shouted reverse and backed away to try again to locate the passage.

After many attempts, he knew it would be impossible to find the passage. All we could do was try to reach the harbor at Apia, forty miles away. We were helpless against the ferocious power of the elements. I do not remember ever being where it was so dark.

We made no progress for the first hour, even though the engine was at full throttle. The boat would struggle up a mountainous wave and then pause in exhaustion at the top of the crest with the propellers out of the water. The vibration of the propellers would shake the boat almost to pieces before it slid down the other side.

We were lying spread-eagled on the cover of the cargo hold, holding on with our hands on one side and with our toes locked on the other to keep from being washed overboard. Brother Mark Littleford lost hold and was thrown against the low iron rail. His head was cut, but the rail kept him from being washed away.

Eventually, we moved ahead and near daylight finally pulled into the harbor at Apia. Boats were lashed to one another for safety. They were several deep at the pier. We crawled across them, trying not to disturb those sleeping on deck. We made our way to Pesega, dried our clothing, and headed for Vailuutai to organize the new stake.

I do not know who had been waiting for us at the beach at Mulifanua. I refused to let them tell me. But it is true that without that lower light, we all might have been lost.

There is in our hymnbook an old and seldom-sung hymn that has very special meaning to me.

> *Brightly beams our Father's mercy*
> *From his lighthouse evermore,*

But to us he gives the keeping
Of the lights along the shore.

Let the lower lights be burning;
Send a gleam across the wave.
Some poor fainting, struggling seaman
You may rescue, you may save.

Dark the night of sin has settled;
Loud the angry billows roar.
Eager eyes are watching, longing,
For the lights along the shore.

Trim your feeble lamp, my brother;
Some poor sailor, tempest-tossed,
Trying now to make the harbor,
In the darkness may be lost.
(Philip Paul Bliss, "Brightly Beams Our
Father's Mercy," *Hymns* [1985], no. 335)

There are those who may be lost and are searching for that lower light to help guide them back. These thoughts are directed to them.

It was understood from the beginning that in mortality we would fall short of being perfect. It was not expected that we would live without transgressing one law or another.

"For the natural man is an enemy to God, and has been from the fall of Adam, and will be, forever and ever, unless he yields to the enticings of the Holy Spirit, and putteth off the

No matter what

our transgressions

have been,

no matter

how much

our actions may have

hurt others,

that guilt can all

be wiped out.

natural man and becometh a saint through the atonement of Christ the Lord" (Mosiah 3:19).

From the Pearl of Great Price, we understand that "no unclean thing can dwell" in the kingdom of God (Moses 6:57), and so a way was provided for all who sin to repent and become worthy of the presence of our Father in Heaven once more.

A Mediator, a Redeemer, was chosen, one who would live His life perfectly, commit no sin, and offer "himself a sacrifice for sin, to answer the ends of the law, unto all those who have a broken heart and a contrite spirit; and unto none else can the ends of the law be answered" (2 Nephi 2:7).

Concerning the importance of the Atonement, in Alma we learn, "For it is expedient that an atonement should be made; . . . or else all mankind must unavoidably perish" (Alma 34:9).

If you have made no mistakes, then you do not need the Atonement. If you have made mistakes—and all of us have, whether minor or serious—then you have an enormous need to find out how they can be erased so that you are no longer in darkness.

"[Jesus Christ] is the light and the life of the world" (Mosiah 16:9). As we fix our gaze on His teachings, we will be guided to the harbor of spiritual safety.

The third article of faith states, "We believe that through the Atonement of Christ, all mankind may be saved, by obedience to the laws and ordinances of the Gospel."

President Joseph F. Smith taught: "Men cannot forgive their own sins; they cannot cleanse themselves from the consequences of their sins. Men can stop sinning and can do right in the future, and so far [as] their acts are acceptable before the Lord [become] worthy of consideration. But who shall repair the wrongs they have done to themselves and to others, which it seems impossible for them to repair themselves? By the atonement of Jesus Christ the sins of the repentant shall be washed away; though they be crimson they shall be made white as wool [see Isaiah 1:18]. This is the promise given to you" (*Teachings of Presidents of the Church: Joseph F. Smith* [1998], 99–100).

We do not know exactly how the Lord accomplished the Atonement. But we do know that the cruel torture of crucifixion was only part of the horrific pain that began in Gethsemane—that sacred site of suffering—and was completed on Golgotha.

Luke records:

"He was withdrawn from them about a stone's cast, and kneeled down, and prayed,

"Saying, Father, if thou be willing, remove this cup from me: nevertheless not my will, but thine, be done.

"And there appeared an angel unto him from heaven, strengthening him.

"And being in an agony he prayed more earnestly: and his sweat was as it were great drops of blood falling down to the ground" (Luke 22:41–44).

So far as I have been able to tell, there is only one account in the Savior's own words that describes what He endured in the Garden of Gethsemane. The revelation records:

"For behold, I, God, have suffered these things for all, that they might not suffer if they would repent;

"But if they would not repent they must suffer even as I;

"Which suffering caused myself, even God, the greatest of all, to tremble because of pain, and to bleed at every pore" (D&C 19:16–18).

Throughout your life there may have been times when you have gone places you never should have gone and done things you never should have done. If you will turn away from sin, you will be able one day to know the peace that comes from following the pathway of complete repentance.

No matter what our transgressions have been, no matter how much our actions may have hurt others, that guilt can all be wiped out. To me, perhaps the most beautiful phrase in all scripture is when the Lord said, "Behold, he who has repented of his sins, the same is forgiven, and I, the Lord, remember them no more" (D&C 58:42).

That is the promise of the gospel of Jesus Christ and the Atonement: to take anyone who comes, anyone who will join, and put them through an experience so that at the end of their life, they can go through the veil having repented of their sins and having been washed clean through the blood of Christ (see Revelation 1:5).

That is what Latter-day Saints do around the world. That is the Light we offer to those who are in darkness and have lost their way. Wherever our members and missionaries may go, our message is one of faith and hope in the Savior Jesus Christ.

President Joseph Fielding Smith wrote the lyrics to the hymn "Does the Journey Seem Long?" He was a dear friend of mine. I close with his encouragement and promise to those who seek to follow the teachings of the Savior:

Does the journey seem long,
The path rugged and steep?
Are there briars and thorns on the way?
Do sharp stones cut your feet
As you struggle to rise
To the heights thru the heat of the day?

Is your heart faint and sad,
Your soul weary within,
As you toil 'neath your burden of care?
Does the load heavy seem
You are forced now to lift?
Is there no one your burden to share?

Let your heart be not faint
Now the journey's begun;
There is One who still beckons to you.
So look upward in joy
And take hold of his hand;
He will lead you to heights that are new—

A land holy and pure,
Where all trouble doth end,
And your life shall be free from all sin,
Where no tears shall be shed,
For no sorrows remain.
Take his hand and with him enter in.
("Does the Journey Seem Long?"
 Hymns [1985], no. 127)

CHAPTER 4

———◦———

"I Will Remember Your Sins No More"

My message is about a father and a son. Alma, the father, was a prophet; his son, Corianton, a missionary.

Two of Alma's sons—Shiblon and Corianton, the youngest—were on a mission to the Zoramites. Alma was greatly disappointed at the failure of his son Corianton to live the standards of a missionary. Corianton forsook his ministry and went to the land of Siron after the harlot Isabel (see Alma 39:3).

"This was no excuse for thee, my son. Thou shouldst have tended to the ministry wherewith thou wast entrusted" (Alma 39:4).

Alma told his son that the devil had led him away (see Alma 39:11). Unchastity is "most abominable above all sins

---

From a talk given at general conference, April 2006.

save it be the shedding of innocent blood or denying the Holy Ghost" (Alma 39:5).

"I would to God that ye had not been guilty of so great a crime." He then said: "I would not dwell upon your crimes, to harrow up your soul, if it were not for your good.

"But behold, ye cannot hide your crimes from God" (Alma 39:7–8).

He sternly commanded his son to accept the counsel of his older brothers (see Alma 39:10).

Alma told him that his iniquity was great because it turned away investigators: "When they saw your conduct they would not believe in my words.

"And now the Spirit of the Lord doth say unto me: Command thy children to do good, lest they lead away the hearts of many people to destruction; therefore I command you, my son, in the fear of God, that ye refrain from your iniquities" (Alma 39:11–12).

After this severe rebuke, Alma the loving father became Alma the teacher. He knew that "the preaching of the word had a great tendency to lead the people to do that which was just—yea, it had had more powerful effect upon the minds of the people than the sword, or anything else" (Alma 31:5). So Alma taught Corianton.

He spoke first of Christ: "My son, I would say somewhat unto you concerning the coming of Christ. Behold, I say unto you, that it is he that surely shall come to take away the sins of the world; yea, he cometh to declare glad tidings of salvation unto his people" (Alma 39:15).

Corianton asked how they could know about the coming of Christ so far in advance.

Alma replied, "Is not a soul at this time as precious unto God as a soul will be at the time of his coming?" (Alma 39:17).

Corianton was "worried concerning the resurrection of the dead" (Alma 40:1).

Alma had inquired of God concerning the Resurrection and told Corianton of the First Resurrection and of other resurrections. "There is a time appointed that all shall come forth from the dead" (Alma 40:4).

He had inquired as to "what becometh of the souls of men from this time of death to the time appointed for the resurrection" (Alma 40:7).

Alma then told Corianton, "All men, whether they be good or evil, are taken home to that God who gave them life" (Alma 40:11). The "righteous are received into a state of happiness" (Alma 40:12), and the evil are "led captive by the will of the devil" (Alma 40:13). The righteous remain "in paradise, until the time of their resurrection" (Alma 40:14).

"Ye cannot say, when ye are brought to that awful crisis, that I will repent, that I will return to my God. Nay, ye cannot say this; for that same spirit which doth possess your bodies at the time that ye go out of this life, that same spirit will have power to possess your body in that eternal world" (Alma 34:34).

Alma told his son "that there is a space between death and the resurrection of the body, and a state of the soul in happiness or in misery until the time which is appointed of God that the dead shall come forth, and be reunited, both soul and body, and be brought to stand before God, and be judged according to their works" (Alma 40:21).

"The soul"—that is, the spirit—"shall be restored to the body, and the body to the soul" (Alma 40:23). "This," he said, "is the restoration of which has been spoken by the mouths of the prophets" (Alma 40:24). Alma said that "some have wrested the scriptures, and have gone far astray because of this thing" (Alma 41:1).

Alma then said: "And now, my son, I perceive there is somewhat more which doth worry your mind, which ye cannot understand—which is concerning the justice of God in the punishment of the sinner; for ye do try to suppose that it is injustice that the sinner should be consigned to a state of misery.

"Now behold, my son, I will explain this thing unto thee" (Alma 42:1–2).

He told Corianton about the Garden of Eden and the Fall of Adam and Eve: "And now, ye see by this that our first parents were cut off both temporally and spiritually from the presence of the Lord; and thus we see they became subjects to follow after their own will" (Alma 42:7).

"It was appointed unto man to die" (Alma 42:6).

He then explained why death is absolutely necessary: "If it were not for the plan of redemption, (laying it aside) as soon as they were dead their souls were miserable, being cut off from the presence of the Lord" (Alma 42:11).

Alma taught Corianton about justice and mercy: "According to justice, the plan of redemption could not be brought about, only on conditions of repentance of men" (Alma 42:13).

He explained that "the plan of mercy could not be brought about except an atonement should be made; therefore God himself atoneth for the sins of the world, to bring about the plan of mercy, to appease the demands of justice, that God might be a perfect, just God, and a merciful God also" (Alma 42:15).

He taught Corianton about the unwavering standard of eternal law (see Alma 42:17–25).

He very bluntly explained why punishment was necessary: "Now, repentance could not come unto men except there were a punishment, which also was eternal as the life of the soul should be, affixed opposite to the plan of happiness, which was as eternal also as the life of the soul" (Alma 42:16).

Alma knew personally the pain of punishment and the joy of repentance. He himself had once greatly disappointed his own father, Corianton's grandfather. He rebelled and went about "seeking to destroy the church" (Alma 36:6). He was struck down by an angel, not because he deserved it but because of the prayers of his father and others (see Mosiah 27:14).

Alma felt the agony and guilt and said: "As I was thus racked with torment, while I was harrowed up by the memory of my many sins, behold, I remembered also to have heard my father prophesy unto the people concerning the coming of one Jesus Christ, a Son of God, to atone for the sins of the world.

"Now, as my mind caught hold upon this thought, I cried within my heart: O Jesus, thou Son of God, have mercy on me, who am in the gall of bitterness, and am encircled about by the everlasting chains of death.

"And now, behold, when I thought this, I could remember

Could there be any sweeter or more

consoling words, more filled with hope, than

those words from the scriptures?

"I, THE LORD, REMEMBER [THEIR SINS] NO MORE."

—D&C 58:42

my pains no more; yea, I was harrowed up by the memory of my sins no more.

"And oh, what joy, and what marvelous light I did behold; yea, my soul was filled with joy as exceeding as was my pain!

"Yea, I say unto you, my son, that there could be nothing so exquisite and so bitter as were my pains. Yea, and again I say unto you, my son, that on the other hand, there can be nothing so exquisite and sweet as was my joy. . . .

"Yea, and from that time even until now, I have labored without ceasing, that I might bring souls unto repentance; that I might bring them to taste of the exceeding joy of which I did taste; that they might also be born of God, and be filled with the Holy Ghost" (Alma 36:17–21, 24).

Alma asked Corianton, "Do ye suppose that mercy can rob justice?" (Alma 42:25). He explained that because of the Atonement of Christ, both could be satisfied by eternal law.

"Moved upon by the Holy Ghost" (D&C 121:43; see also Alma 39:12), he had rebuked Corianton with sharpness. Then, after plainly, patiently teaching these fundamental principles of the gospel, there came the abundance of love.

The Prophet Joseph Smith was taught through revelation that "no power or influence can or ought to be maintained by virtue of the priesthood, only by persuasion, by long-suffering, by gentleness and meekness, and by love unfeigned;

"By kindness, and pure knowledge, which shall greatly enlarge the soul without hypocrisy, and without guile—

"Reproving betimes with sharpness, when moved upon by the Holy Ghost; and then showing forth afterwards an increase of love toward him whom thou hast reproved, lest he esteem thee to be his enemy;

"That he may know that thy faithfulness is stronger than the cords of death" (D&C 121:41–44).

Alma said: "O my son, I desire that ye should deny the justice of God no more. Do not endeavor to excuse yourself in the least point because of your sins, by denying the justice of God; but do you let the justice of God, and his mercy, and his long-suffering have full sway in your heart; and let it bring you down to the dust in humility" (Alma 42:30).

Corianton's grandfather, also named Alma, was among the priests who had served the wicked King Noah. He heard Abinadi the prophet testify of Christ, and he was converted. Condemned to death, he fled the evil court to teach of Christ (see Mosiah 17:1–4).

Now Alma, in turn, was the father pleading with his son Corianton to repent.

After sternly rebuking his son and patiently teaching the doctrine of the gospel, Alma the loving father said, "And now, my son, I desire that ye should let these things trouble you no more, and only let your sins trouble you, with that trouble which shall bring you down unto repentance" (Alma 42:29).

In agony and shame, Corianton was brought "down to the dust in humility" (Alma 42:30).

Alma, who was Corianton's father and also his priesthood leader, was now satisfied with Corianton's repentance. He lifted the terrible burden of guilt his son carried and sent him back to the mission field: "And now, O my son, ye are called of God to preach the word unto this people. . . . Go thy way, declare the word with truth and soberness. . . . And may God grant unto you even according to my words" (Alma 42:31).

Corianton joined his brothers, Helaman and Shiblon, who were among the priesthood leaders. Twenty years later in the land northward, he was still faithfully laboring in the gospel (see Alma 49:30; 63:10).

It is a wicked, wicked world in which we live and in which our children must find their way. Challenges of pornography, gender confusion, immorality, child abuse, drug addiction, and all the rest are everywhere. There is no way to escape from their influence.

Some are led by curiosity into temptation, then into experimentation, and some become trapped in addiction. They lose hope. The adversary harvests his crop and binds them down.

Satan is the deceiver, the destroyer, but his is a temporary victory.

The angels of the devil convince some that they are born to a life from which they cannot escape and are compelled to live in sin. The most wicked of lies is that they cannot change and repent and that they will not be forgiven. That cannot be true. They have forgotten the Atonement of Christ.

"For, behold, the Lord your Redeemer suffered death in the flesh; wherefore he suffered the pain of all men, that all men might repent and come unto him" (D&C 18:11).

Christ is the Creator, the Healer. What He made, He can fix. The gospel of Jesus Christ is the gospel of repentance and forgiveness (see 2 Nephi 1:13; 2 Nephi 9:45; Jacob 3:11; Alma 26:13–14; Moroni 7:17–19).

"Remember the worth of souls is great in the sight of God" (D&C 18:10).

The account of this loving father and a wayward son, drawn from the Book of Mormon: Another Testament of Jesus Christ, is a type, a pattern, an example.

Each of us has a loving Father in Heaven. Through the Father's redeeming plan, those who may stumble and fall "are not cast off forever" (Book of Mormon title page).

"And how great is his joy in the soul that repenteth!" (D&C 18:13).

"The Lord cannot look upon sin with the least degree of allowance; nevertheless" (D&C 1:31–32), the Lord said, "he who has repented of his sins, the same is forgiven, and I, the Lord, remember them no more" (D&C 58:42).

Could there be any sweeter or more consoling words, more filled with hope, than those words from the scriptures? "I, the Lord, remember [their sins] no more" (D&C 58:42). That is the testimony of the Book of Mormon, and that is my testimony to you.

Part Two

THE
HOLY GHOST
AND
REVELATION

CHAPTER 5

The Gift of the Holy Ghost

My purpose is to teach you through doctrine and scripture why it is that we do things as we do. I will give some direction and suggestions as to how we can do things better in order that each member of the Church will be thoroughly converted and never will fall away.

Joseph Smith said: "You might as well baptize a bag of sand as a man, if not done in view of the remission of sins and getting of the Holy Ghost. Baptism by water is but half a baptism, and is good for nothing without the other half—that is, the baptism of the Holy Ghost" (*History of the Church of Jesus Christ of Latter-day Saints,* 7 vols. [1932–51], 5:499).

Preparing people for baptism without teaching about the gift of the Holy Ghost would be like holding a sacrament

From a talk given at a seminar for new mission presidents, June 24, 2003. See Ensign, *August 2006, 46–52.*

meeting in which only the bread was blessed and passed. They would receive but half.

We will discuss linking baptism in an absolutely tight relationship to confirmation and the conferring of the gift of the Holy Ghost.

Confirmation and Conferring the Gift of the Holy Ghost

Confirmation has two parts: to confirm as a member of the Church, and then to confer the gift of the Holy Ghost. The priesthood holder performing that ordinance "bestows the gift of the Holy Ghost by saying, 'Receive the Holy Ghost'" (*Family Guidebook* [pamphlet, 2001], 20).

There are two visible examples of the manifestations of the Holy Ghost I know of in the scriptures. The first was when the Lord was baptized:

"And Jesus, when he was baptized, went up straightway out of the water: and, lo, the heavens were opened unto him, and he saw the Spirit of God descending like a dove, and lighting upon him" (Matthew 3:16; see also 1 Nephi 11:27; 2 Nephi 31:8; D&C 93:15).

The other example came on the day of Pentecost. The Apostles had no doubt been ordained, but the Lord had now left them. They wondered what to do. They remembered He told them to stay in Jerusalem, and so they obeyed. And then it happened. They were in a house, and there was "a sound from heaven as of a rushing mighty wind, and it filled all the house where they were sitting.

"And there appeared unto them cloven tongues like as of fire, and it sat upon each of them.

"And they were all filled with the Holy Ghost" (Acts 2:2–4). Then they were authorized; they were prepared.

Then they could move about in the ministry that the Lord had called and commissioned them to do.

In the Doctrine and Covenants that pattern was repeated when the Lord said:

"Thou didst baptize by water unto repentance, but they received not the Holy Ghost;

"But now I give unto thee a commandment, that thou shalt baptize by water, and they shall receive the Holy Ghost by the laying on of the hands, even as the apostles of old" (D&C 35:5–6).

When Paul went to Ephesus he found twelve men who had been baptized, but they had not yet received the Holy Ghost. They said to Paul, "We have not so much as heard whether there be any Holy Ghost" (Acts 19:2).

What happened next is significant. Paul had them baptized again. Then he conferred upon them, by the laying on of hands, the gift of the Holy Ghost (see Acts 19:2–7).

Remember the fourth article of faith: "The first principles and ordinances of the Gospel are: first, Faith in the Lord Jesus Christ; second, Repentance; third, Baptism by immersion for the remission of sins; fourth, Laying on of hands for the gift of the Holy Ghost."

When parents are teaching their children and when missionaries are teaching investigators, preparing them for baptism by water, they must also think of the gift of the Holy

Ghost—baptism by fire. Think of it as one sentence: First comes the baptism of water and then the baptism of fire.

Someone may ask the missionaries, "How are things going?" or "Are you teaching anyone?"

The missionaries automatically answer, "Yes, we have a family preparing for baptism and confirmation, for *receiving the Holy Ghost.*"

Or a father and mother might say to a child, "When you are eight years old, you will be ready to be baptized and *receive the Holy Ghost.*"

I repeat, *to be baptized* and *to receive the Holy Ghost*—link those two together.

All I say is evident and outlined in section 20 of the Doctrine and Covenants (see vv. 41–43, 45, 68). There are also some other references where this message is affirmed (see Acts 8:12, 14–17; D&C 33:11, 15; 36:2; 39:23; 49:13–14; 55:1; 68:25; 76:51–52; Articles of Faith 1:4).

Joseph Smith said, "The baptism of water, without the baptism of fire and the Holy Ghost attending it, is of no use; they are necessarily and inseparably connected" (*History of the Church,* 6:316).

"And it came to pass when they were all baptized and had come up out of the water, the Holy Ghost did fall upon them, and they were filled with the Holy Ghost and with fire" (3 Nephi 19:13).

An excerpt from another verse teaches that this will come "if it so be that ye believe in Christ, and are baptized, first with water, then with fire and with the Holy Ghost, following the example of our Savior" (Mormon 7:10).

Again, there are *two* parts to baptism—baptism by water and baptism by fire or the Holy Ghost. If you separate the two, as the Prophet Joseph Smith said, it is but half a baptism.

Communication from the Holy Ghost

How does the Holy Ghost communicate?

There is an example in 1 Nephi chapter 17 where Laman and Lemuel had been brutal to Nephi. They, in fact, had tried to take his life. In due course, he said to them:

"Ye are swift to do iniquity but slow to remember the Lord your God. Ye have seen an angel, and he spake unto you; yea, ye have heard his voice from time to time; and he hath spoken unto you *in a still small voice,* but ye were past *feeling,* that ye could not *feel* his words" (1 Nephi 17:45; emphasis added).

That communication seldom comes audibly. Most of the time it comes through your *feelings,* as it did in this case.

In another example, the Lord taught this principle to Joseph Smith and Oliver Cowdery: "But, behold, I say unto you, that you must study it out in your mind [work, study]; then you must ask me if it be right, and if it is right I will cause that your bosom shall burn within you [the fire, burn]; therefore, you shall *feel* that it is right" (D&C 9:8; emphasis added). This applies to all of us.

Speaking with the Tongue of Angels

"Wherefore, my beloved brethren, I know that if ye shall follow the Son, with full purpose of heart, acting no hypocrisy and no deception before God, but with real intent, repenting of your sins, witnessing unto the Father that ye are willing to take upon you the name of Christ, by baptism—yea, by following your Lord and your Savior down into the water, according to his word, behold, then shall ye receive the Holy Ghost; yea, then cometh the baptism of fire and of the Holy Ghost." Now this important principle: "And *then can ye speak with the tongue of angels,* and shout praises unto the Holy One of Israel.

"But, behold, my beloved brethren, thus came the voice of the Son unto me, saying: After ye have repented of your sins, and witnessed unto the Father that ye are willing to keep my commandments, by the baptism of water, and have received the baptism of fire [that is the conferring] of the Holy Ghost, [ye] can speak with a new tongue, yea, even with the tongue of angels" (2 Nephi 31:13–14; emphasis added).

Nephi gives a clear explanation of what happens after baptism and confirmation and the reception of the Holy Ghost:

"Wherefore, do the things which I have told you I have seen that your Lord and your Redeemer should do; for, for this cause have they been shown unto me, that ye might know the gate by which ye should enter. For the gate by which ye should enter is repentance and baptism by water [which is a symbolic witness of repentance]; and then cometh [the promise of cleansing for] a remission of your sins by fire and by the Holy Ghost" (2 Nephi 31:17).

We sometimes speak of baptism for the remission of sins. The remission, if you will read the scriptures carefully, comes through the baptism of fire and of the Holy Ghost.

"And now, behold, my beloved brethren, I suppose that

PREPARING PEOPLE FOR BAPTISM

without teaching about

THE GIFT OF THE

HOLY GHOST

would be like holding a sacrament
meeting in which only the bread was
blessed and passed.

ye ponder somewhat in your hearts concerning that which ye should do after ye have entered in by the way." Here are people who have been baptized and received the Holy Ghost, and they wonder what they are to do. Nephi answers: "But, behold, why do ye ponder these things in your hearts?

"Do ye not remember that I said unto you that after ye had received the Holy Ghost ye could speak with the tongue of angels? And now, how could ye speak with the tongue of angels save it were by the Holy Ghost?

"Angels speak by the power of the Holy Ghost; wherefore, they speak the words of Christ. Wherefore, I said unto you, feast upon the words of Christ; for behold, the words of Christ will tell you all things what ye should do" (2 Nephi 32:1–3).

Everything that missionaries are to know and to do is to bring their investigators to understand both baptism and confirmation. Then the investigators have their agency. Consider these simple words:

"Wherefore, now after I have spoken these words, if ye cannot understand them it will be because ye ask not, neither do ye knock; wherefore, ye are not brought into the light, but must perish in the dark.

"For behold, again I say unto you that if ye will enter in by the way, and *receive the Holy Ghost*, it will show unto you *all things* what ye should do.

"Behold, this is the doctrine of Christ, and there will be no more doctrine given until after he shall manifest himself unto you in the flesh" (2 Nephi 32:4–6; emphasis added).

Now you must understand that baptism by water, as the Prophet Joseph Smith said plainly, is but half a baptism. Paul, when the Ephesian converts had not received the Holy Ghost, started over again (see Acts 19:2–7).

"For behold, again I say unto you that if ye will enter in by the way, and receive the Holy Ghost, it will show unto you all things what ye should do" (2 Nephi 32:5).

You can receive this great blessing—to become familiar with the still small voice and learn that this voice will tell you all things that you must do. The word we use to describe this communication is *promptings,* the way we *feel.* These promptings can come many times, through many experiences. That is the voice of the Lord speaking.

"Angels speak by the power of the Holy Ghost; wherefore, they speak the words of Christ" (2 Nephi 32:3).

Nephi explained that angels speak by the power of the Holy Ghost, and you can speak with the tongue of angels, which simply means that you can speak with the power of the Holy Ghost. It will be quiet. It will be invisible. There will not be a dove. There will not be cloven tongues of fire. But the power will be there.

Opposition by the Adversary

One word of warning: There is also a spirit of opposition and evil. That warning can also be found in the scriptures:

"But whatsoever thing persuadeth men to do evil, and believe not in Christ, and deny him, and serve not God, then ye may know with a perfect knowledge it is of the devil; for after this manner doth the devil work, for he persuadeth no man to do good, no, not one; neither do his angels; neither do they who subject themselves unto him" (Moroni 7:17).

The spiritual communications from the Holy Ghost can be interrupted by the promptings and influence of the evil one. You will learn to recognize that.

To further our understanding of this principle, Nephi taught:

"And now, my beloved brethren, I perceive that ye ponder still in your hearts; and it grieveth me that I must speak concerning this thing. For if ye would hearken unto the Spirit which teacheth a man to pray ye would know that ye must pray; for the evil spirit teacheth not a man to pray, but teacheth him that he must not pray.

"But behold, I say unto you that ye must pray" (2 Nephi 32:8–9).

So when we speak of angels communicating by the power of the Holy Ghost and we are told by the prophets that we can speak with the tongue of angels, then we must know that there is an opposing influence. We must be able to detect it.

There is one word in the book of Jacob that should alert us:

"Behold, will ye reject these words? Will ye reject the words of the prophets; and will ye reject all the words which have been spoken concerning Christ, after so many have spoken concerning him; and deny the good word of Christ, and the power of God, and the gift of the Holy Ghost, and *quench* the Holy Spirit, and make a mock of the great plan of redemption?" (Jacob 6:8; emphasis added).

So the Spirit can be quenched!

Discerning Spiritual Experiences

When you receive these special spiritual experiences, they are not to be chattered about. They are private, and they are personal. You will come to know with a very personal conviction that the Lord knew you were coming that way.

You may learn by trial and error and say, "I *knew* I shouldn't have done that. I knew I shouldn't have!" How did you know? Because you knew. You were being *prompted.*

Or you will say regretfully, "I knew I should have done that and didn't." How will you know? You are being worked upon by the Spirit.

Promptings may come as "sudden strokes of ideas" (*History of the Church,* 3:381).

"I will tell you in your mind and in your heart, by the Holy Ghost" (D&C 8:2).

"Put your trust in that Spirit which leadeth to do good—yea, to do justly, to walk humbly, to judge righteously; and this is my Spirit.

" . . . I will impart unto you of my Spirit, which shall enlighten your mind, which shall fill your soul with joy;

"And then shall ye know, or by this shall you know, all things whatsoever you desire of me, which are pertaining unto things of righteousness, in faith believing in me that you shall receive" (D&C 11:12–14).

"Did I not speak peace to your mind concerning the matter? What greater witness can you have than from God?" (D&C 6:23).

Conversion

Conversion does not always happen immediately. Nevertheless, it comes as a quiet thing. It is a still small voice. There are these very interesting verses in the book of Alma, and you will come to know what this means:

"Therefore, blessed are they who humble themselves without being compelled to be humble; or rather, in other words, blessed is he that believeth in the word of God, and is *baptized without stubbornness of heart,* yea, without being brought to know the word, or even compelled to know, before they will believe.

"Yea, there are many who do say: If thou wilt show unto us a sign from heaven, then we shall know of a surety; then we shall believe" (Alma 32:16–17; emphasis added).

Investigators may say: "It looks right and feels right. I still don't know about it. It just feels good." Reason is prompting them, and they are baptized without stubbornness of heart. So the conversion comes.

Others may say: "You talk about this gift of the Holy Ghost and baptism by fire. Show me! Give me the witness, and then I will be baptized."

For some it will take time. They may be disappointed when you say: "You will know *after* you decide! It takes an exercise of faith. You may not know at first and have that firm conviction, but it will come."

The Word of Wisdom

Surely you can understand where the Word of Wisdom fits into this. How significant it is, "given for a principle with promise, adapted to the capacity of the weak and the weakest of all saints, who are or can be called saints" (D&C 89:3).

This principle comes with a promise: "Run and not be weary, . . . walk and not faint" (D&C 89:20). That is desirable.

But there is a more important promise: "And shall find wisdom and great treasures of knowledge, even hidden treasures" (D&C 89:19).

Can you see the necessity of the Word of Wisdom? We press our people, almost beg our people, to behave themselves, to keep their spiritual person in tune so that they can have the reception of the Holy Ghost. Your body is the instrument of your mind and spirit. You must take proper care of it.

Never Will Fall Away

If people are properly taught, they never will fall away:

"And as sure as the Lord liveth [that is an oath], so sure as many as believed, or as many as were brought to the knowledge of the truth, through the preaching of Ammon and his brethren, according to the spirit of revelation and of prophecy, and the power of God working miracles in them—yea, I say unto you, as the Lord liveth [a second oath], as many of the Lamanites as believed in their preaching, and were converted unto the Lord, *never did fall away*" (Alma 23:6; emphasis added).

Those who have been taught and who receive the gift of the Holy Ghost, the baptism of fire, will never fall away. They will be connected to the Almighty, who will guide them in their lives.

The Comforter

You never need to feel or be alone:

"And I will pray the Father, and he shall give you another Comforter, that he may abide with you for ever; . . .

"I will not leave you comfortless: I will come to you" (John 14:16, 18).

"Yea, verily, verily, I say unto you, that the field is white already to harvest; wherefore, thrust in your sickles, and reap with all your might, mind, and strength.

"Open your mouths and they shall be filled.

"Yea, open your mouths and spare not, and you shall be laden with sheaves upon your backs, for lo, I am with you"(D&C 33:7–9).

The baptismal prayer given in the Book of Mormon states:

"And now behold, these are the words which ye shall say, calling them by name, saying:

"Having authority given me of Jesus Christ, I baptize you in the name of the Father, and of the Son, and of the Holy Ghost. Amen" (3 Nephi 11:24–25).

I bear witness of these words and of these Names. I invoke the blessings of the Lord upon you as an Apostle of the Lord Jesus Christ to the end that His Spirit will be with you, and you will understand and can move forward accompanied by that power of the Holy Ghost.

CHAPTER 6

Prayer and
Promptings

No Father would send His children off to a distant, dangerous land for a lifetime of testing where Lucifer was known to roam free without first providing them with a personal power of protection. He would also supply them with means to communicate with Him from Father to child and from child to Father. Every child of our Father sent to earth is provided with the Spirit of Christ, or the Light of Christ (see D&C 84:46). We are none of us left here alone without hope of guidance and redemption.

The Restoration began with the prayer of a fourteen-year-old boy and a vision of the Father and the Son. The dispensation of the fulness of times was ushered in.

The Restoration of the gospel brought knowledge of the premortal existence. From the scriptures, we know of the

---

From a talk given at general conference, October 2009.

Council in Heaven and the decision to send the sons and daughters of God into mortality to receive a body and to be tested (see D&C 138:56; see also Romans 8:16). We are children of God. We have a spirit body housed, for now, in an earthly tabernacle of flesh. The scriptures say, "Know ye not that ye are the temple of God, and that the Spirit of God dwelleth in you?" (1 Corinthians 3:16).

As children of God, we learn we are part of His "great plan of happiness" (Alma 42:8).

We know that there was a War in Heaven and that Lucifer and those who followed him were cast out without bodies:

"Satan, that old serpent, even the devil, . . . rebelled against God, and sought to take the kingdom of our God and his Christ—

"Wherefore, he maketh war with the saints of God, and encompasseth them round about" (D&C 76:28–29).

We were given our agency (see D&C 101:78). We must use it wisely and remain close to the Spirit; otherwise, we foolishly find ourselves yielding to the enticements of the adversary. We know that through the Atonement of Jesus Christ our mistakes can be washed clean, and our mortal body will be restored to its perfect frame.

"For behold, the Spirit of Christ is given to every man, that he may know good from evil; wherefore, I show unto you the way to judge; for every thing which inviteth to do good, and to persuade to believe in Christ, is sent forth by the power and gift of Christ; wherefore ye may know with a perfect knowledge it is of God" (Moroni 7:16).

There is a perfect manner of communication through the

Spirit, "for the Spirit searcheth all things, yea, the deep things of God" (1 Corinthians 2:10).

Following baptism into The Church of Jesus Christ of Latter-day Saints, there comes a second ordinance: "Laying on of hands for the gift of the Holy Ghost" (Articles of Faith 1:4).

That sweet, quiet voice of inspiration comes more as a feeling than it does as a sound. Pure intelligence can be spoken into the mind. The Holy Ghost communicates with our spirits through the mind more than through the physical senses (see 1 Corinthians 2:14; D&C 8:2; 9:8–9). This guidance comes as thoughts, as feelings through promptings and impressions (see D&C 11:13; 100:5). We may *feel* the words of spiritual communication more than *hear* them, and we *see* them with spiritual rather than with mortal eyes (see 1 Nephi 17:45).

I served for many years in the Quorum of the Twelve Apostles with Elder LeGrand Richards. He died at the age of ninety-six. He told us that as a boy of twelve he attended a great general conference in the Tabernacle. There he heard President Wilford Woodruff speak.

President Woodruff told of an experience of being prompted by the Spirit. He was sent by the First Presidency to "gather all the Saints of God in New England and Canada and bring them to Zion" (in Conference Report, April 1898, 30).

He stopped at the home of one of the brethren in Indiana and put his carriage in the yard, where he and his wife and one child went to bed while the rest of the family slept in the house. Shortly after he had retired for the night, the Spirit whispered, warning him, "Get up, and move your carriage." He got up and moved the carriage a distance from where it had stood. As he was returning to bed, the Spirit spoke to him again: "Go and move your mules away from that oak tree." He did this and then retired once again to bed.

Not more than thirty minutes later, a whirlwind caught the tree to which his mules had been tied and broke it off at the ground. It was carried a hundred yards through two fences. The enormous tree, which had a trunk five feet in circumference, fell exactly upon the spot where his carriage had been parked. By listening to the promptings of the Spirit, Elder Woodruff had saved his life and the lives of his wife and child (see Wilford Woodruff, *Leaves from My Journal* [1881], 88).

That same Spirit can prompt you and protect you.

When I was first called as a General Authority, we lived on a very small plot of ground in Utah Valley that we called our farm. We had a cow and a horse and chickens and lots of children.

One Saturday, I was to drive to the airport for a flight to a stake conference in California. But the cow was expecting a calf and in trouble. The calf was born, but the cow could not get up. We called the veterinarian, who soon came. He said the cow had swallowed a wire and would not live through the day.

I copied the telephone number of the animal by-products company so my wife could call them to come and get the cow as soon as she died.

Before I left, we had our family prayer. Our little boy said our prayer. After he had asked Heavenly Father to "bless Daddy in his travels and bless us all," he then started an earnest plea. He said, "Heavenly Father, please bless Bossy cow so that she will get to be all right."

PURE INTELLIGENCE

can be spoken into the mind.

The Holy Ghost

COMMUNICATES WITH OUR

SPIRITS THROUGH THE MIND

MORE THAN THROUGH THE

PHYSICAL SENSES.

In California, I told of the incident and said, "He must learn that we do not get everything we pray for just that easily."

There was a lesson to be learned, but it was I who learned it, not my son. When I returned Sunday night, Bossy had "got to be all right."

This process is not reserved for the prophets alone. The gift of the Holy Ghost operates equally with men, women, and even little children. It is within this wondrous gift and power that the spiritual remedy to any problem can be found.

"And now, he imparteth his word by angels unto men, yea, not only men but women also. Now this is not all; little children do have words given unto them many times, which confound the wise and the learned" (Alma 32:23).

The Lord has many ways of pouring knowledge into our minds to prompt us, to guide us, to teach us, to correct us, to warn us. The Lord said, "I will tell you in your mind and in your heart, by the Holy Ghost, which shall come upon you and which shall dwell in your heart" (D&C 8:2).

And Enos recorded, "While I was thus struggling in the spirit, behold, the voice of the Lord came into my mind again" (Enos 1:10).

You can know the things you need to know. Pray that you will learn to receive that inspiration and remain worthy to receive it. Keep that channel—your mind—clean and free from the clutter of the world.

Elder Graham W. Doxey, who once served in the Second Quorum of the Seventy, told me of an experience. His mother, who was later a counselor in the Primary general presidency, also told me of this experience.

During World War II, he was in the navy posted to China. He and several others went by train to the city of Tientsin to look around.

Later they boarded a train to return to their base, but after more than an hour, the train turned north. They were on the wrong train! They spoke no Chinese. They pulled the emergency cord and stopped the train. They were put off somewhere in the countryside with nothing to do but walk back to the city.

After walking for some time, they found a small pump-handle car, the kind that the railroad workers use. They set it on the rails and began to pump their way along the tracks. It would coast downhill, but it had to be pushed uphill.

As they came to one steep downhill slope, they scrambled aboard the car and began to coast. Graham was the last to get aboard. The only place left for him was in the front of the car. He ran alongside and finally started to climb aboard. As he did so, he slipped and fell. He was bouncing on his back with his feet against the car to keep from being run over. As the car quickly gained speed, he heard his mother's voice say, "Bud, you be careful!"

He wore heavy military boots. His foot slipped, and the thick sole of his boot caught in a gear of a wheel and stopped the car just one foot from his hand.

His parents, who were presiding over the East Central States Mission at the time, were sleeping in a hotel room. His mother sat up at about two o'clock in the morning and awakened her husband, saying: "Bud's in trouble!" They knelt by the bed and prayed for the safety of their boy.

The next letter he received said, "Bud, what's wrong? What happened to you?"

He then wrote to tell them what had happened. When they compared times, at the very time he was bouncing along that track, his parents were on their knees in the hotel room half a world away, praying for his safety.

These experiences of prompting and prayer are not uncommon in the Church. They are part of the revelation our Heavenly Father has provided for us.

One of the adversary's sharpest tools is to convince us that we are no longer worthy to pray. No matter who you are or what you may have done, you can always pray.

When temptation comes, you can invent a delete key in your mind—perhaps the words from a favorite hymn. Your mind is in charge; your body is the instrument of your mind. When some unworthy thought pushes into your mind, replace it with your delete key. Worthy music is powerful and can help you control your thoughts (see D&C 25:12).

When Oliver Cowdery failed in an attempt to translate, the Lord told him:

"Behold, you have not understood; you have supposed that I would give it unto you, when you took no thought save it was to ask me.

"But, behold, I say unto you, that you must study it out in your mind; then you must ask me if it be right, and if it is right I will cause that your bosom shall burn within you; therefore, you shall feel that it is right.

"But if it be not right you shall have no such feelings" (D&C 9:7–9).

That principle is illustrated by the story of a little girl. She was upset with her brother, who built a trap to catch sparrows.

Unable to get help to stop him, she said to herself, "Well, I'll pray about it."

After her prayer, the little girl told her mother, "I know he is not going to catch any sparrows in his trap because I prayed about it. I'm *positive* he won't catch any sparrows!"

Her mother said, "How can you be so sure?"

She said, "After I prayed about it, I went out and kicked that old trap all to pieces!"

Pray even if you are young and wayward like the prophet Alma or have a closed mind like Amulek, who "knew concerning these things, yet . . . would not know" (Alma 10:6).

Learn to pray. Pray often. Pray in your mind, in your heart. Pray on your knees. Prayer is your personal key to heaven. The lock is on your side of the veil. And I have learned to conclude all my prayers with "Thy will be done" (Matthew 6:10; see also Luke 11:2; 3 Nephi 13:10).

Do not expect to be free entirely from trouble and disappointment and pain and discouragement, for these are the things that we were sent to earth to endure.

Someone wrote:

> *With thoughtless and impatient hands*
> *We tangle up the plans*
> *The Lord hath wrought.*

And when we cry in pain He saith,
"Be quiet, man, while I untie the knot."
(Author unknown, in Jack M. Lyon et al.,
Best-Loved Poems of the LDS People [1996], 304)

The scriptures promise, "There hath no temptation taken you but such as is common to man: but God is faithful, who will not suffer you to be tempted above that ye are able; but will with the temptation also make a way to escape, that ye may be able to bear it" (1 Corinthians 10:13).

I conclude with a promise from the Savior Himself: "Draw near unto me and I will draw near unto you; seek me diligently and ye shall find me; ask, and ye shall receive; knock, and it shall be opened unto you" (D&C 88:63).

CHAPTER 7

"And They Knew It Not"

The Church of Jesus Christ did not begin with the First Vision. We must go centuries before to learn of the beginning of the Church of Jesus Christ. The gospel had existed from all eternity. In the Doctrine and Covenants we find the expression "from before the world was" (D&C 124:38), speaking of the priesthood and the principles of the gospel.

We will begin on the banks of the Jordan River. John the Baptist, who had been in the wilderness of Judea, was there baptizing. He was asked, "Are you the Messiah?" He said, "I am not the Messiah" (see John 1:20). "I . . . baptize you with water unto repentance: but he that cometh after me . . . shall baptize you with the Holy Ghost, and with fire" (Matthew 3:11).

From a talk given at a Church Educational System fireside, March 5, 2000, Utah Valley State College.

Then came Jesus from Judea to John to be baptized. John protested and said, "I have need to be baptized of thee" (Matthew 3:14). Christ was baptized, and the scriptures record that:

"The heavens . . . opened . . . and . . . the Spirit of God [descended in the form of] a dove, and [lighted] upon him:

"And . . . a voice from heaven [said], This is my beloved Son, in whom I am well pleased" (Matthew 3:16–17).

Christ went from His baptism into the wilderness to fast, and there Satan came tempting Him (see Matthew 4:1–2). There is a great lesson for all of us in what transpired next. When He faced Perdition himself, three times He was confronted, and each time He deflected the power of the adversary with simple verses of scripture. "Man shall not live by bread alone" (Matthew 4:4). "Thou shalt not tempt the Lord thy God" (Matthew 4:7). "Thou shalt worship the Lord thy God, and him only shalt thou serve" (Matthew 4:10). Now, there is a great lesson.

If you read the New Testament, you find, "It is written" all throughout Christ's teaching of His Apostles. They would ask Him questions, and He would say, "Have you not read the scriptures, which say . . ." (see Matthew 12:3, 5; 19:4; Mark 12:10, 26; Luke 6:3; 3 Nephi 27:5); or He would say, "It was said by them in times of old . . ." (see Matthew 5:21, 27, 33; 3 Nephi 12:21); or on many occasions, when He was confronted with problems or challenges, He would simply say, "It is written," and quote the scriptures (see Matthew 4:4, 7, 10; 21:13; 26:24; 26:31; Mark 1:2; 7:6; 9:12, 13; 14:21, 27;

Luke 4:4, 8, 27; 7:27; 19:46; 24:46; John 6:31, 45; 3 Nephi 12:7, 33, 38, 43).

We do not ask that everyone in the Church be a scriptorian, but all of us should have a constant and continuous knowledge of the scriptures and the revelations. It should be ever growing.

After Christ had returned from that great cleansing preparation, He began to teach His disciples and those who followed Him. Everywhere He went He caused great interest, and always there was great opposition. In due time, as Luke records, after spending all night in prayer, He called to Him His disciples, and of them He chose twelve whom He also named Apostles.

He ordained them Apostles, and during His ministry His effort was to teach them. If you will read, for instance, the tenth chapter of Matthew, it is addressed to the Twelve as He taught them. It is interesting, too, that He was often correcting them, on occasion rebuking them. Frequently it was because they did not seem to know what they should know or what seemed to be obvious.

Eventually, His teaching of the Twelve and His ministry on earth were drawing to a close, and He kept giving signals of that end to His Twelve. Either they could not or they did not want to face the reality that He was going to leave them. But He spoke of the Comforter and of the gift of the Holy Ghost. "The Comforter," He said, would "teach [them] all things, and bring all things to [their] remembrance, whatsoever [He had] said unto [them]" (John 14:26).

When it was obvious that He was going to His death, the

Apostles were with Him, and Peter protested. Peter said, "I'll go with you," meaning he would give his life. And again, the Lord corrected him and said, "You don't understand. If I don't go, I cannot give you the gift, the gift of the Holy Ghost." That could not be given until after He was glorified (see John 16:7).

And so the day came when they saw Him on the cross.

Later, He appeared to them in resurrected form and taught them more about what they were to do. His challenge to them was to go to all the world, to teach the gospel to every nation, kindred, tongue, and people, and to baptize in the name of the Lord (see Matthew 28:19).

I can imagine how helpless they felt, because I understand how helpless we feel when we look at the tremendous responsibility that is placed upon the Church.

He had been with them, and He taught them, and then before He left them, He told them to "[linger] in . . . Jerusalem, until [you are] endued [or clothed] with power from [the Father]" (Luke 24:49). And then He ascended. You remember that as they watched, two men stood by and said, "Why stand ye gazing up into heaven? this same Jesus, which [ye see ascend will] come [again]" (Acts 1:11).

The promise that they would be endowed or clothed with power was not long in coming. The Apostles were gathered in a house on the day of the Pentecost, a great Jewish celebration, and suddenly, in the room where they were gathered, there was a sound of great rushing of wind. And then "cloven tongues like as of fire" (Acts 2:3) descended and lighted on every one of them, and they received the Holy Ghost (see Acts 2:2–4). The gift of the Holy Ghost then was with the Apostles.

The Prophet Joseph Smith said there is a difference between the gift of the Holy Ghost and the Holy Ghost. The Holy Ghost operates, and has operated through the centuries, on many who have not been in the Church (see *Teachings of the Prophet Joseph Smith* [1976], 199); but the gift of the Holy Ghost was the gift that He gave the Apostles, and He told them to confer it upon all who would believe and be baptized.

Can you imagine these humble Apostles? The Pharisees were not very impressed with them. These twelve men were described as "unlearned and ignorant men" (Acts 4:13). But they did what they were called to do. They went abroad to preach in all the world. They went, as we suppose, to India, to places east. We know they went to Egypt and to all of the known civilized world, building up the Church and ordaining and teaching—ordaining bishops, as we know. And always in fear, I suppose, of their mortal lives. Most of them were martyred. Paul and Peter both died in about A.D. 64 in Rome. But the Church had been established, and the priesthood was upon the earth. The Apostles were there.

As the years rolled on, the light that was there—the light typified by the cloven tongues of fire—began to flicker, then dim.

In due time, there were great men who were determined to keep the light of Christ alive. Athanasius was responsible, more than any other one man, for collecting the New Testament as we know it. There were other great men, saintly men, who were leading the Church.

Then Constantine—the great Roman Emperor who is supposed to have saved the Church when persecution was such that it literally was not worth one's life to be a Christian—took over the Church. He was the one who called the first councils. Then there moved into the inner circle the influence of scholars and so-called intellectuals. There came then what we now know as the Apostasy.

Much they had was right and true. I have great reverence for those who came a little later who knew things were not right. They knew that it was not as it should be—Luther, Calvin, Zwingli, Knox, Tyndale, and others who literally paid with their lives trying to correct things. A number of them died as martyrs too—burned at the stake. The Reformation had begun, but to reform what was left was not enough.

We know that the boy Joseph went into the Sacred Grove. He had read in the New Testament that:

"If any of you lack wisdom, let him ask of God, that giveth to all men liberally, and upbraideth not; and it shall be given him.

"But let him ask in faith, nothing wavering. For he that wavereth is like a wave of the sea driven with the wind and tossed" (James 1:5–6).

I can understand why it began with a fourteen-year-old boy. There was no sophistication there. He just was simple enough to believe it. So, appraising himself and saying to himself, "Well, if anybody lacks wisdom, it's me," he went into the woods, and there he knelt.

And then it happened. The powers of darkness fell upon him, and he explained, "This wasn't an imaginary power, but the power of a real being from the unseen world who had such marvelous power as never before had I felt in any being." He was about to abandon himself. And then he used a key. He called upon the name of Christ—the name, *the name!* And when he had done so, a light descended, and when it fell upon him the darkness vanished, as it must (see Joseph Smith—History 1:10–17).

Darkness cannot persist in the presence of light. That is another principle that you should know. You can demonstrate that physically. I know how to wire a dark room from a source of power, put in a switch, and turn the light on—and darkness will vanish. I do not know, and I do not know anybody who does know, how to put darkness into a room and make light vanish.

As we look back at the history of the Church with Joseph Smith and his beginning, the word *Restoration* came—a restoring of the gospel or a bringing forward a fulness of the gospel as it had existed in the time of Christ.

The gospel was revealed, and the Church was organized, bit by bit. They did not get it all at once. I am sure they were very puzzled. They didn't know quite what to do about baptism. They didn't know quite what to do about authority. There had been some illustrations of how that worked.

The Wesleys in England knew that they had to do something to organize a church, so John or Charles Wesley ordained a man by the name of Thomas Coke as bishop. Someone wrote and published:

So easily are Bishops made
By man's, or woman's whim?
Wesley his hands on Coke hath laid,
But who laid hands on him?
(John R. Tyson, ed., *Charles Wesley:*
A Reader [1989], 429)

And that's the puzzle.

John the Baptist came and conferred upon Joseph and Oliver the keys of the Aaronic Priesthood, which holds the keys of the ministering of angels (remember that) unto baptism by immersion for the remission of sins. But there was no laying on of hands for the gift of the Holy Ghost there, because that authority does not attend the Aaronic Priesthood. That was in 1829 (see D&C 13).

About that same time, the next great visitation took place when Peter, James, and John appeared and conferred upon the Prophet Joseph Smith and others the Melchizedek Priesthood, "the priesthood . . . after the holiest order of God" (D&C 84:18), "*the Holy Priesthood, after the Order of the Son of God*" (D&C 107:3; italics in original).

Interestingly enough, the scriptures do not say much about exactly when that took place or how it took place. There is just a verse that said it had already taken place, that Joseph Smith was an Apostle (see D&C 20:2).

The Church was organized in 1830. They set about to baptize. A revelation came, actually to Sidney Rigdon, who was baptizing. The Lord made a correction. He said, "You are baptizing in water," and then He compared it to the baptism

DARKNESS
CANNOT PERSIST
in the presence of
LIGHT.

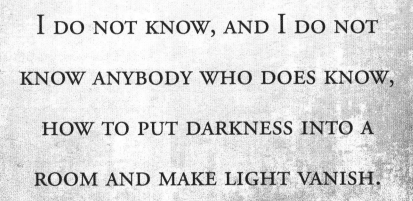

I DO NOT KNOW, AND I DO NOT
KNOW ANYBODY WHO DOES KNOW,
HOW TO PUT DARKNESS INTO A
ROOM AND MAKE LIGHT VANISH.

of John and said that from then on, "[You are to confer] the Holy Ghost by the laying on of the hands, [as did] the apostles of old" (D&C 35:6; see also vv. 4–6). And they had learned something new.

On January 5, about a month later, another revelation came, which affirmed that there was to accompany each baptism the laying on of hands for the gift of the Holy Ghost (see D&C 39:23). From then on into our day that has been the process.

And here we are in our day. We have had the Holy Ghost conferred upon us. I quote now the sentence from which my title is taken: "And they knew it not."

The Lord said to the Nephites, "Whoso cometh unto me with a broken heart and a contrite spirit [shall receive baptism] with fire and with the Holy Ghost, even as the Lamanites . . . were baptized with fire and with the Holy Ghost, and they knew it not" (3 Nephi 9:20).

Can you imagine that? I think every one of us at times, and many of us all the time, have no appreciation or understanding of the gift of the Holy Ghost. We have the power and authority that comes with that gift. As you read the revelations, you will find the Holy Ghost referred to as a comforter (think of that—a comforter) and as a teacher, and we are told that it will abide with us and be in us.

In Paul's letter to Timothy, he prophesied: "In the last days perilous times shall come. For men shall be lovers of their own selves, covetous, boasters, proud, blasphemers, . . . without natural affection, . . . heady, highminded" (2 Timothy 3:1–4).

We live in a day when the moral and spiritual values of

the world are pretty tough. We *could* look forward with great yearning and hope that things will get better. But they are not going to get better! The trend that is happening all around us—in society and government and education and all else—is a continuous trend.

And yet with all of that, I stand with great hope and great optimism. I have no fear. Fear is the antithesis of faith. With all that is happening and with all the impossible challenges that we face, we have that supernal gift of the Holy Ghost conferred upon us. And yet, for the most part, we know it not. It's interesting how in our lives we are operating, to an extent, as though we had not received it.

You can take a light globe, put a couple of wires on it, bare the ends of the wires, put the globe in the socket, and take it to a high-tension wire. Just holding it up near the insulation, it can draw enough power to make that light turn on just a little. That is the way we are. We have so much that is available, and we shouldn't fear!

The marvelous thing is that this light, this gift, operates with every one of us in our own lives. The Lord has not required that all of us choose the same occupation or be the same size, weight, age, or anything else. Whosoever will come with a contrite spirit and a broken heart will receive the baptism of fire and the Holy Ghost (see 3 Nephi 9:20). It is conferred equally on men and women.

The prophet Mormon asked, "Has the day of miracles ceased? Or have angels ceased to appear [and minister] unto the children of men? . . . Or will [they], so long as time shall last, or the earth shall stand, or there shall be one man upon the face thereof to be saved?" (Moroni 7:35–36).

And the answer: "Behold I say unto you, Nay; for . . . if these things have ceased, then has faith ceased also; and awful is the state of man, for they [would be] as though there had been no redemption made" (Moroni 7:37–38).

Did you know that the Lord told His Twelve that it is not only their privilege but their responsibility to perform miracles as needed, and that they were one of the signs? We don't seek after signs, but they are attendant to the authority, and they are attendant in our day.

Read the scriptures. I know that the matter of reading the scriptures and doing it in a systematic way becomes very difficult in our busy lives, but if you will be reading in them all the time and getting the feel for them, you will have the Spirit. Which scripture? It doesn't matter. Just find yourself in the scriptures—the revelations—reading. And begin asking for the Holy Ghost to inspire you and guide you.

The message that is most repeated in all of the revelations is said in many ways but always expressed simply: "Ask, and ye shall receive." I counted them once. There were more than seven hundred different ways of saying, "Ask, and ye shall receive."

The Lord said, "Behold, I stand at the door, and knock: if any man hear my voice, and open the door, I will come in to him, and will sup with him" (Revelation 3:20).

You likely know the famous painting of Christ at the door holding a lantern. It is said that one little boy pointed out, "There is no latch on the door." And the painter said, "The painting is accurate. That is the heart's door. It opens only from within."

You will not be forced! Change your life and admit the inspiration of the Holy Ghost. Begin to get your feelings sensitive enough so that you can be guided. You will not be denied!

As we move forward in the Church into these perilous times, we can move forward with a heart that is full of faith, with certainty, with a power, with a feeling. As you begin to ask and to cultivate the Spirit, you will find little packages along the way, little bits of information, little circumstances that are not coincidental. And you will know that He knows that you are coming along that way.

Sometimes it will be a sign that says "don't." How long has it been since you have said to yourself, "I knew I shouldn't have done that! I just knew I shouldn't have done that!" Well, how long has it been since you looked back and said, "I knew I should have done that!"

You have in your *feelings* the beacon and the guide, and it will help you in all walks of life. If you have not studied, it will not help you in a test to try to remember something that you did not know in the first place. There is the necessity of laboring in life.

I do know that against challenges and difficulties that come, if you will invite that Spirit, that gift, to be with you and teach you, then you have the right to have all of the blessings that anyone else in the Church has, including those of us who preside over the Church. I do not hold any more priesthood than any elder in the Church. The priesthood is not divisible. There are different offices and different responsibilities, but each of us should have the spirit of prophecy and revelation as it relates to our own lives.

We should be able to see what is ahead. As we begin to test our feelings, it is a case of trial and error.

If you fall and stumble, you pick yourself up and repent and move forward. You will find that the gospel is true, the simple truth. And you will know it. You will know it for yourself, and it will be individual, and you will not need to worry.

I remember sending some elders over to Harvard University to meet with a professor who was going to entertain himself at the expense of a couple of our missionaries. They begged me to go with them. I didn't want to go. I didn't want to face Harvard professors! If I had gone, I would have robbed the elders of an important experience. I knew that.

I said, "You just go. I know they will belittle you and ridicule your beliefs. Just remember, bear your testimony; just bear your testimony."

Well, interesting! One young man particularly—who was from a little town in southern Utah, hardly old enough in maturity to be a missionary—went there with great fear.

The next morning they came into my office. They were walking on air above the floor, speaking figuratively.

I said, "What happened?"

He said, "We confounded them! We confounded them!"

You do not need to fear. Be a Latter-day Saint.

When I was in the military, I was put together with a group of young men up at Washington State University. There were about ten of us in an apartment in Stimpson Hall. We were there for some special pilot training. The others began to introduce themselves. I was at the end of the row. As they went around the circle, I began to shrink. They had all been to college except me. I had barely escaped from high school. One of them mentioned that each summer his family had gone on "the Continent." I didn't know that meant they had gone to Europe. Another one was a son of a man who had been governor of Ohio and at that time was one of the cabinet members in the federal government. All of them, it seemed to me, had everything to recommend them, and I had nothing.

It came me, and I said, "I come from a little town in northern Utah that you have never heard of. My dad runs a garage. I come from a big family, and we have the blessings of the Church." I said another thing or two.

To my great surprise, I was accepted. They didn't care that my father wasn't a member of the president's cabinet or that our family hadn't gone on "the Continent." I learned something. Since that time I have had no fear of meeting people of high station—or any people—and I have felt the confidence that comes when you have the gift of the Holy Ghost.

I do know, because the scriptures tell us, that when a man speaks with the power of the Holy Ghost, the power of the Holy Ghost will carry it into the hearts of those that listen (see 2 Nephi 33:1).

Go forward without fear. Do not fear the future. Do not fear whatever is ahead of you. Take hold of that supernal gift of the Holy Ghost. Learn to be taught by it. Learn to call upon it. Learn to live by it. And the Spirit of the Lord will attend you, and you will be blessed as it was intended that we should all be blessed by this gift.

I bear witness that God lives, that Jesus is the Christ. This is His Church. I know that. I know the Lord. I know that as He taught in Judea and Galilee in those ancient days, He made the way that the gift of the Holy Ghost could be established then and reclaimed and restored in our day. It will never be taken again from the earth. It rests with each of us who is a member of the Church.

CHAPTER 8

———◦○◦———

The 20-Mark Note

Over thirty years ago I was assigned with then-Elder Thomas S. Monson to organize a servicemen's stake in Europe. We met at Berchtesgaden, Germany, high in the Bavarian Alps. Originally it was a headquarters built by Adolf Hitler in an incomparably beautiful place. Seldom has there been on this earth anyone who has duplicated in personality and purpose the adversary quite as much as did Adolf Hitler. I thought that we had come full circle where that had taken place on that site, and now we were gathered there to organize a stake of Zion.

After we had finished setting apart and completing that organization, we were assigned to go to Berlin for a stake conference. We needed to get from Berchtesgaden high in the Alps down to Munich to the airport.

From a talk given at a Brigham Young University—Idaho devotional, March 12, 2002. See New Era, *June 2009, 2–6.*

We got to the airport in ample time for our plane, which was scheduled to leave at about ten o'clock in the morning, but it was fogged in. We sat there listening to the announcements for nearly twelve hours. They kept saying they thought the fog would clear. It did not clear.

That *night* near ten o'clock, two missionary elders came to the airport. We knew then that the planes would not fly. They told us there was a train leaving Munich for Berlin at midnight. The elders took us to the train station, helped us buy our tickets, and saw us aboard the train, which would take from about midnight until about ten the next morning to arrive in Berlin.

As the train was pulling out, one young elder said, "Do you have any German money?"

I shook my head no.

He said, "You better have some," and, running alongside, pulled from his pocket a 20-mark note. He handed that to me.

At that time the Iron Curtain was very "iron." The train stopped at Hof on the border between West Germany and East Germany, and the crews were changed. All of the West German crew members got off the train, and the East German crew got on the train. Then the train set out across East Germany toward Berlin.

The U.S. government had just begun to issue five-year passports. I had a new passport, a five-year passport. Before our trip, we went to have my wife's passport renewed, but they sent it back saying that the three-year passports were honored as a five-year passport. According to that reckoning, she still had two years left on her passport.

At about two o'clock in the morning, a conductor, a military-type soldier, came and asked for our tickets, and then, noting that we were not German, he asked for our passports. I do not like to give up my passport, especially in unfriendly places. But he took them. I almost never dislike anybody, but I made an exception for him! He was a surly, burly, ugly man.

We spoke no German. In the train compartment, there were six of us: me, my wife, and a German sitting to the side of her, and then almost knee to knee in a bench facing us were three other Germans. We had all been conversing a little. When the conductor came in, all was silent.

A conversation took place, and I knew what he was saying. He was denying my wife's passport. He went away and came back two or three times.

Finally, not knowing what to do, I had a bit of inspiration and produced that 20-mark note. He looked at it, took the note, and handed us our passports.

The next morning when we arrived in Berlin, a member of the Church met us at the train. I rather lightly told him of our experience. He was suddenly very sober. I said, "What's the matter?"

He said, "I don't know how to explain your getting here. East Germany right now is the one country in the world that refuses to honor the three-year passport. To them, your wife's passport was not valid."

I said, "Well, what could they have done?"

He answered, "Put you off the train."

I said, "They wouldn't put us off the train, would they?"

He said, "Not *us*. Her!"

I could see myself having someone try to put my wife off the train at two o'clock in the morning somewhere in East Germany. I am not sure I would know what to do. I did not learn until afterwards how dangerous it was and what the circumstances were, particularly for my wife. I care a good deal more about her than I do for myself. We had been in very serious danger. Those whose passports they would not accept were arrested and detained.

Our Lives Are Guided

All of this comes to this point: the elder who handed me the 20-mark note was David A. Bednar, a young elder serving in the South German Mission, who is now a member of the Quorum of the Twelve Apostles.

So why was it that this young elder from San Leandro, California, handed me the 20-mark note? If you understand that and understand what life is about, you will understand really all you need to know about life as a member of the Church. You will understand how our lives are really not our own. They are governed—and if we live as we should live, then we will be taken care of. I do not think he knew the consequences of what he was doing. That 20-mark note was worth six dollars, and six dollars to an elder is quite a bit!

As you go through life, you will find that these things happen when you are living as you ought to live.

If you can learn what the Spirit is, then you never need to be alone. In Doctrine and Covenants 46:2, it says, "Notwithstanding those things which are written, it always has been

OUR LIVES

are really not our own.

THEY ARE GOVERNED—

and if we live as

we should live, then

WE WILL BE

TAKEN CARE OF.

given to the elders of my church from the beginning, and ever shall be, to conduct all meetings as they are directed and guided by the Holy Spirit."

Your Spirit Body

The doctrine explained in the scriptures, the revelations, tells us that we are dual beings. We know there is a spirit and a body. "The spirit and the body [when they are eternally combined, become] the soul of man" (D&C 88:15). So there are two parts of you. There is a spirit inside of a body.

You have a spirit body; your intelligence existed forever (see D&C 93:29). That is hard to get through your mind. We are going to live forever. You believe that, don't you? In the Resurrection, we will live eternally. That cannot be unless that is true of the past, too, that we lived eternally in the past. We are in the middle of something eternal here.

I have wondered about when the day comes that my spirit leaves my body. When that "unwrapping" takes place and your body is set aside and we are looking at your spirit, what are you going to look like? What will your spirit look like?

Some of you might be described as perfect athletes—perfectly coordinated, able to do anything! You have beautiful physical bodies. If we separated your body from your spirit, what would your spirit look like? You will learn, if you will study and pray and feel, that you could have a beautiful body and a shriveled, weak spirit. On the other hand, you can have a body that is limited in many ways, and yet in the eternal scheme of things, you can train and teach your spirit so that it becomes of imperishable worth.

You can look forward to the day when you are "unwrapped" and your spirit is separated from the body. Your spirit is young and vibrant and beautiful. Even if your body is old and diseased or crippled or disabled in any way, when the spirit and body are put together in the Resurrection, then you will be glorious; then you will be glorified.

A man I knew—one of the great men I have known—was in his childhood one of a bunch of roustabout boys. They were always where they should not be and never where they should be. Finally, a wise, resourceful leader got them into a Sunday School class. The teacher was an old man—just an ordinary, homely old man. More than that, he was a convert from Europe, and he did not speak English very well. They giggled, "Our teacher? Him?" These boys, I suppose, had the reputation of running any teacher out.

Then my friend said that something happened. The teacher started to speak, and they all began to listen. This friend said, "You could warm your hands by the fire of his faith." That meant that in that older, worn-out body that did not seem to be able to erase an accent, there was a powerful spirit.

In the Resurrection the body—the dust of the earth, the carnal part of us—can be renewed and made powerful if it is to equal the spirit.

The Holy Ghost Will Guide You

If you can understand how the Spirit operates, you will be all right. There is not enough evil put together—if it was all brought together as some kind of a dark, ugly laser beam and focused on you, it could not destroy you, unless somehow you consented to it.

In the course of your learning, "wisdom is the principal thing; therefore get wisdom: and with all thy getting get understanding" (Proverbs 4:7).

Make sure you learn the things that you are not taught overtly. If all you know is what you read or what you can hear, you will not know very much. Moments of reverence are so precious when you *think* and *feel.* That is why temples are so important. You can go to the temple and be out of the world.

The promise from the Lord is that when you receive the Holy Ghost, "he shall teach you all things, and bring all things to your remembrance, whatsoever I have said unto you" (John 14:26).

You will be doing some things automatically, almost unwittingly. Without thinking, you will find you have been prompted and guided by the Holy Spirit. That is why this young elder, without knowing why, took a 20-mark note out of his wallet as he was trotting alongside the train and handed it to me as the train was pulling out. He saved us from great danger.

That is how you will do things and then later look back and know that you were guided. And also that is how you will be warned. You will be warned, "Don't go there! Don't do that!" You will be warned, "Don't go with him! Don't go with her! Don't be with them!" And then, "Do be in this company!" You will be guided, and the Lord will watch over you.

I know that the gospel is true, that Jesus is the Christ, that He lives, that this is His Church. Find a place in the world where you can, without embarrassment, without any hesitancy, declare to yourself: first, that you accept the gospel of Jesus Christ, and second, that what you *are* is more important than what you *do*. What you do, if it is guided, will make you what you *are* and what you can *be*.

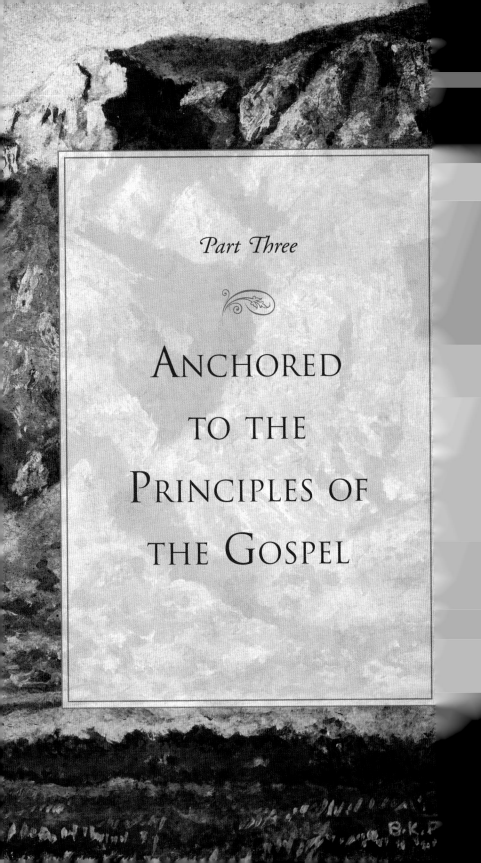

Part Three

Anchored to the Principles of the Gospel

CHAPTER 9

A Faithful Heritage

Some years ago, I met with a group of Saints in Iowa who had gathered to honor the handcart pioneers who stopped in that area for carts and provisions—flour, salt, sugar, and other things—to sustain them while crossing 1,200 miles of wilderness. They were already abundantly provisioned with faith, determination, and a deep spiritual fire that burned inside of them.

Why did they come? First let me tell you some of *what* they did, then finish the *why*. I will tell you about my great-grandmother, Christena Olsen Wight.

In June of 1851, a mob wrecked the meetinghouse of a little branch of the Church in Aalborg, Denmark, and then went from one member's home to another, wrecking each of them. The mayor of the town said that he could not protect

---

From a talk given at a handcart pioneer commemoration fireside, June 11, 2006, University of Iowa.

them; they must leave (see Christena Olsen Wight, unpublished diary, 1; transcript in possession of author).

Mostly they came to the Salt Lake Valley as families. The father, Christen Olsen, and the mother, Anne, could not get enough money to bring their whole family. They sent fourteen-year-old James ahead in 1853, and in 1854, with three younger children, the parents left Denmark, leaving three teenage girls—Christena, Nicoline, and Caroline—to follow when they could. It took the girls three years to earn the money. In 1857, the sisters came on the steamer *Westmoreland*, which was five weeks in crossing the ocean to Philadelphia, and then on to Iowa City (see Wight, 1–2; see also C. C. A. Christensen, "By Handcart to Utah: The Account of C. C. A. Christensen," *Nebraska History,* Winter 1985, 336).

Here they bought supplies and a handcart. The record says, "We were only allowed to take with us fifteen pounds in weight for each person who was to travel with the handcarts, and that included our tinware for eating, bedding, and any clothing we did not wish to carry ourselves" (Christensen, "By Handcart to Utah," 337).

Caroline was so happy to be in the safety of this country that she bought a metal American flag pin. She wore it proudly all her life. They headed west with the seventh company of handcarts (see Wight, 2, 6).

Let me quote from the diary of my great-grandmother: "At night the tents were pitched. We cooked our meal on the campfire. . . . We had to gather buffalo chips for firewood. We baked biscuits [each night] for the next day. Our food was running low. We had only three biscuits a day . . . , one for each meal. At Fort Laramie we didn't have any flour left. Now we had just one biscuit a day and still had to walk all day and pull the cart. . . . I sewed the biscuit in the hem of my dress so I would not have to carry it" (Wight, 3–4).

Food was very scarce. One old Danish man, who had lost his sense of smell, came into camp with what he thought would make a good soup. He had killed it with his cane. It was a skunk! They evacuated the camp for a while (see Christensen, "By Handcart to Utah," 342).

A fourth girl was assigned to the Olsen sisters' handcart. That extra girl came down with typhoid fever and had to be pulled and pushed most of the way (see Wight, 3).

In Iowa City, Christena had purchased three pairs of shoes—enough, she thought, to see her across the plains. Two pairs were worn out long before they got to Fort Laramie. The last pair she tied around her neck with a string. She was not going to walk into the valley barefooted (see Wight, 3, 5).

In that company was a sixty-year-old woman from Norway. Totally blind, she walked 1,200 miles across the prairies and across the Rockies on the arm of her daughter. "She was always cheerful. . . . We could often hear her merry laughter when she unexpectedly found herself wading through one . . . of the many streams. . . . 'Now, Mother, we are about to cross some water,' we could hear her daughter warning her, 'Is it deep?' or 'How deep is it?' we heard in reply from the blind woman; and when the explanation was satisfactory, she walked cheerfully out into the water" (Christensen, "By Handcart to Utah," 338–39).

Then Christena wrote: "Three times in one day we waded

across the Platte River. The second time we had to cross, Nicoline and I pushed and pulled our handcart, trying to cross. I pushed with all the strength that I had and I said, 'If I have to cross that river again today, I will never make it.' I didn't have strength to do it again. I prayed and prayed that I would not have to cross that river again that day. Just before nightfall, we came to the Platte River again. When we got there some of the people were already across on the other side. We pulled our handcart into the river. When we got to the middle of the stream our strength failed us since the water was so swirl[ing]. We and our cart started to float away downstream. I had no strength left to fight the stream and cart. I said to myself as I was floating down the stream, 'This is such a heavenly peaceful feeling I could just float on to heaven. Now I will not have to push and pull this heavy cart anymore.' There were deep holes and quicksand in the swirl water. We were close to the point of drowning when a young man, Christiensen Anus (who was our captain of ten handcarts), came to our rescue and helped us across the river. He saved our lives" (Wight, 4).

"After 70 days on the trail . . . we were all suffering greatly for the want of water. Our thirst became unbearable. . . . One out of ten of our company died . . . and never made it to Salt Lake Valley" (Wight, 5).

One morning as they broke camp, a woman came holding something in her apron. It was a baby born to her in the night. She had walked all day in the sun the day before and intended to walk that day. They had her ride instead. Incidentally, both mother and baby survived (see Christensen, "By Handcart to Utah," 340).

WE KNOW
why
WE ARE HERE
AND
where
WE ARE GOING.

When they broke camp "early in the morning, generally, the children who could walk—some even under the age of four—were sent ahead, accompanied by [some of the] sisters, partly to avoid the dust and partly to walk as far as possible before the burning sun and exhaustion would make it necessary to put them in the handcart" (Christensen, "By Handcart to Utah," 339).

Some of the most touching and tragic moments in the history of the Church accompanied these handcart pioneers. One company was commanded by a Brother McArthur.

Archer Walters, an English convert who was with the company, recorded in his diary: "Brother Parker's little boy, age six, was lost. The father went back to hunt him" (in LeRoy R. Hafen and Ann W. Hafen, *Handcarts to Zion: The Story of a Unique Western Migration, 1856–1860* [1960], 61).

The boy, Arthur, was next youngest of four children of Robert and Ann Parker. Three days earlier the company had hurriedly made camp in the face of a sudden thunderstorm. It was then the boy was missed. The parents had thought him to be playing along the way with the other children. Someone remembered earlier in the day, when they had stopped, that they had seen the little boy settle down to rest under the shade of some brush.

You who have little children know how quickly a tired little six-year-old can fall asleep on a sultry summer day, so soundly that even the noise of the camp moving on might not awaken him.

For two days the company remained, and all of the men

searched for him. Then, reluctantly, on July 2, with no choice, the company was ordered west.

Robert Parker, as the diary records, went back alone to search for his little son. As he was leaving camp, his wife pinned a bright shawl about his shoulders and said, "If you find him dead, wrap him in the shawl to bury him. If you find him alive, you could use this as a flag to signal us." She, with the other little children, took the handcart and struggled along with the company (see Hafen and Hafen, *Handcarts to Zion*, 64).

Out on the trail each night, Ann Parker kept watch. At sundown on July 5, she saw a figure approaching from the east! Then in the rays of the setting sun, she saw the glimmer of the bright red shawl.

Under the date of July 5, Brother Walters recorded: "Brother Parker brings into camp his little boy that had been lost. Great joy through the camp. The mother's joy I can not describe" (Hafen and Hafen, *Handcarts to Zion*, 61).

Another diary recorded: "The brave little mother sank, in a pitiful heap in the sand," and that night, for the first time in six nights, she slept (Hafen and Hafen, *Handcarts to Zion*, 64).

We do not know all of the details. A nameless woods-man—I've often wondered how unlikely it was that a woodsman should be there—found the little boy and described him as being sick with illness and with terror, and he cared for him until his father found him.

The handcart pioneers would sing "Come, Come, Ye Saints" as they marched along. It was an anthem for them. One of the verses says, hopefully:

We'll find the place which God for us prepared,
Far away in the West,
Where none shall come to hurt or make afraid;
There the Saints will be blessed.
(*Hymns* [1985], no. 30)

And as they sang, they could see across the Platte River the sun glinting on the weapons of Johnston's Army—2,000 men on their way to the Utah Territory to quash a nonexistent rebellion (see Christensen, "By Handcart to Utah," 342–43). The sending of that army was known afterwards as Buchanan's Blunder.

Although the handcart pioneers suffered terribly, they did not lose hope. When they were almost out of provisions, they arrived at Fort Laramie, 400 miles east of Salt Lake City. "We were met by wagons with flour and fruit, which benefited us greatly, . . . particularly since these wagons picked up the weakest and sickest among us and thus lightened considerably the responsibility for the rest of us" (Christensen, "By Handcart to Utah," 343).

Christena wrote: "That last day's journey, as I woke up in the morning there was a little snow on the ground. I sat down on a rock to take my shoes from around my neck, which I had carried most of the way. I tried to put on my shoes but my feet were so swollen and cut that shoes would not go on. I had to walk into Salt Lake Valley still carrying my shoes like I had for so many hundreds of miles. I walked into the Valley barefooted and with each step I took I left bloody footprints in the snow. We arrived in the Valley on September 13, 1857.

Our very long journey had ended, it took all I had to endure the journey. We rested a few days in Salt Lake and then we went on to Brigham City to see our parents and be with them" (Wight, 5).

Later in life, Christena wrote: "I suffered from body weakness brought on by the strenuous pulling. I suffered all the rest of my life with problems. . . . My stomach was always bad and I had to always watch what I ate, . . . *but I never complained about it.* . . . Nicoline suffered with bad health also" (Wight, 5; emphasis added).

C. C. A. Christensen, who led that company, wrote: "None but those who have experienced such a trial of patience, faith, and endurance can form an idea of what it meant to pull a handcart, which frequently even threatened to collapse because of the extreme heat and lack of humidity, which could cause the [wood of the] cart to split and thus deprive them of the last means they possessed to bring with them their absolute necessities" (Christensen, "By Handcart to Utah," 344).

C. C. A. Christensen became famous as a painter. He painted large canvases of scenes from handcart life. He put them on a roller. He would travel through the settlements and hold meetings. The roll would be suspended, and as he would unroll the canvas by lantern light, he would tell of the experiences illustrated in his paintings. Those paintings of the handcart pioneers are one of the treasures of American art.

Some years later, a visitor to the Salt Lake Valley apologized to Church President George Albert Smith for the Saints having been driven from the pleasant scenes of Europe and the East into the western wilderness to the Utah desert.

President Smith replied, "No, No! You don't understand. We came here willingly—because we *had to!*" (see Conference Report, April 1948, 11–17).

The "had to" part was not because of persecutions or mobbings or even the 2,000 soldiers sent after them. The "had to" was because of what was inside of them. They *knew* why they came.

They knew that there had been a restoration of the fulness of the gospel of Jesus Christ. They knew from the revelations to expect such treatment. They had firm, unshakable, individual testimonies of the life and death and Resurrection of Jesus Christ. They knew that the authority of the priesthood had been restored to earth by angelic messengers. With it came "the same organization that existed in the Primitive Church, namely, apostles [and] prophets" (Articles of Faith 1:6).

They knew that they were fulfilling the prophecy of Isaiah: "And it shall come to pass in the last days, that the mountain of the Lord's house shall be established in the top of the mountains, and shall be exalted above the hills; and all nations shall flow unto it.

"And many people shall go and say, Come ye, and let us go up to the mountain of the Lord, to the house of the God of Jacob; and he will teach us of his ways, and we will walk in his paths: for out of Zion shall go forth the law, and the word of the Lord from Jerusalem" (Isaiah 2:2–3).

Nothing could deter them. They had then, as we have now, individual testimonies, witnesses of the truth of the gospel of Jesus Christ.

Now the fulness of the gospel has spread across the earth.

Today tens of thousands of messengers—missionaries—carry the message of the gospel. They represent millions of members with authority to baptize, ordain, and seal. That is why they came!

In ways, our journey today is harder than theirs and infinitely more dangerous. There are dark, ominous clouds ahead. Each one of us needs, and each can have, the same courage, the same assurance from the same source, the same testimony of the Risen Lord. We know why we are here and where we are going. God bless the pioneers for what they earned for us.

CHAPTER 10

---◦◦◦---

The Test

It is my purpose to show that in troubled times the Lord has always prepared a safe way ahead. We live in those "perilous times" which the Apostle Paul prophesied would come in the last days (see 2 Timothy 3:1–7). If we are to be safe individually and as families, and secure as a church, it will be through "obedience to the laws and ordinances of the Gospel" (Articles of Faith 1:3).

On July 24, 1849, the Saints had been in the valley two years to the day. They finally were free from years of mobbing and persecution. That called for a great celebration.

Just a few years earlier, under dreadful conditions, the Prophet Joseph Smith suffered in Liberty Jail for months while the mobs drove the Saints from their homes. (The words *liberty* and *jail* do not fit together very well.)

From a talk given at general conference, October 2008.

Joseph called out: "O God, where art thou? And where is the pavilion that covereth thy hiding place? How long shall thy hand be stayed, and thine eye, yea thy pure eye, behold from the eternal heavens the wrongs of thy people and of thy servants, and thine ear be penetrated with their cries?" (D&C 121:1–2).

The Prophet Joseph Smith had earlier sought direction, and the Lord told the Saints to seek redress from the judges, the governor, and then the president (see D&C 101:86–88).

Their appeals to the judges failed. During his life, Joseph Smith was summoned to court more than two hundred times on all kinds of trumped-up charges. He was never convicted.

When they sought redress from Governor Boggs of Missouri, he issued a proclamation: "The Mormons must be treated as enemies and *must be exterminated* or driven from the state, if necessary for the public good" (quoted in Joseph Smith, *History of the Church of Jesus Christ of Latter-day Saints,* 7 vols. [1932–51], 3:175).

That unleashed untold brutality and wickedness.

They appealed to President Martin Van Buren of the United States, who told them, "Your cause is just, but I can do nothing for you" (quoted in Eliza R. Snow Smith, *Biography and Family Record of Lorenzo Snow* [1884], 77).

I will read the final paragraphs of their third petition addressed to the Congress of the United States:

"The afflictions of your memorialists have already been overwhelming, too much for humanity, too much for American citizens to endure without complaint. We have groaned under the iron hand of tyranny and oppression these many years.

111

We have been robbed of our property to the amount of two millions of dollars. We have been hunted as the wild beasts of the forest. We have seen our aged fathers who fought in the Revolution, and our innocent children, alike slaughtered by our persecutors. We have seen the fair daughters of American citizens insulted and abused in the most inhuman manner, and finally, we have seen fifteen thousand souls, men, women, and children, driven by force of arms, during the severities of winter, from their sacred homes and firesides, to a land of strangers, penniless and unprotected. Under all these afflicting circumstances, we imploringly stretch forth our hands towards the highest councils of our nation, and humbly appeal to the illustrious Senators and Representatives of a great and free people for redress and protection.

"Hear! O hear the petitioning voice of many thousands of American citizens who now groan in exile . . . ! Hear! O hear the weeping and bitter lamentations of widows and orphans, whose husbands and fathers have been cruelly martyred in the land where the proud eagle . . . floats! Let it not be recorded in the archives of the nations, that . . . exiles sought protection and redress at your hands, but sought it in vain. It is in your power to save us, our wives, and our children, from a repetition of the bloodthirsty scenes of Missouri, and thus greatly relieve the fears of a persecuted and injured people, and your petitioners will ever pray" (quoted in Snow, *Biography*, 152–53).

There was no pity, and they were turned away.

In 1844, while under the avowed protection of Governor Thomas Ford of Illinois, the Prophet Joseph Smith and his brother Hyrum were shot to death in Carthage Jail. Words cannot express the brutality and suffering the Saints had endured.

Now, on this 24th of July in 1849, free at last from the mobbings, they planned to celebrate (see Snow, *Biography,* 95–107).

Everything the Saints owned would come across a thousand miles of desert by handcart or covered wagon. It would be twenty more years before the railroad came as far as Salt Lake City. Even with almost nothing to work with, they determined that the celebration would be a grand expression of their feelings.

They built a bowery on Temple Square. They erected a flagpole 104 feet tall. They made an enormous national flag sixty-five feet in length and unfurled it at the top of this liberty pole.

It may seem puzzling, incredible almost beyond belief, that for the theme of this first celebration they chose patriotism and loyalty to that same government which had rejected and failed to assist them. What could they have been thinking of? If you can understand why, you will understand the power of the teachings of Christ.

Their brass band played as President Brigham Young led a grand procession to Temple Square. He was followed by the Twelve Apostles and the Seventy.

Then followed twenty-four young men dressed in white pants; black coats; white scarves on their right shoulders; coronets, or crowns, on their heads; and sheathed swords at their left sides. In his right hand, of all things, each carried a copy of the Declaration of Independence and the Constitution of the United States. The Declaration of Independence was read aloud by one of those young men.

Next came twenty-four young women dressed in white, blue scarves on their right shoulders and white roses on their heads. Each carried a Bible and a Book of Mormon.

Almost but not quite as amazing as their choice of patriotism for a theme was what came next: twenty-four aged sires (as they were called) led by patriarch Isaac Morley. They were known as the Silver Greys—all sixty years of age or older. Each carried a staff painted red with white ribbon floating at the top. One carried the Stars and Stripes. These men were a symbol of the priesthood, which was "from the beginning before the world was" (D&C 76:13) and had been restored in this dispensation.

The Saints knew that the Lord had told them to be "subject to kings, presidents, rulers, and magistrates, in obeying, honoring, and sustaining the law" (Articles of Faith 1:12). That commandment, revealed then, is true now of our members in every nation. We are to be law-abiding, worthy citizens.

The Lord told them, "I established the Constitution of this land, by the hands of wise men whom I raised up unto this very purpose" (D&C 101:80).

And in another verse, the Lord told them that "it is not right that any man should be in bondage one to another" (D&C 101:79). They were therefore antislavery. This was a very sore spot with the settlers in Missouri.

And so on that day of celebration in 1849, "Elder Phineas Richards came forward in behalf of the twenty-four aged sires, and read their loyal and patriotic address" (Snow, *Biography*, 100). He spoke of the need for them to teach patriotism to

IN

TROUBLED

TIMES

THE LORD

has always prepared

A SAFE WAY AHEAD.

their children and to love and honor freedom. After he briefly recited the perils that they had come through, he said:

"Brethren and friends, we who have lived to three-score years, have beheld the government of the United States in its glory, and know that the outrageous cruelties we have suffered proceeded from a corrupted and degenerate administration, while the pure principles of our boasted Constitution remain unchanged. . . .

" . . . As we have inherited the spirit of liberty and the fire of patriotism from our fathers, so let them descend [unchanged] to our posterity" (quoted in Snow, *Biography,* 102–4).

One would think that, compelled by the force of human nature, the Saints would seek revenge, but something much stronger than human nature prevailed.

The Apostle Paul explained: "The natural man receiveth not the things of the Spirit of God: for they are foolishness unto him: neither can he know them, because they are spiritually discerned. . . . We have the mind of Christ" (1 Corinthians 2:14, 16).

That Spirit defined those early members of the Church as followers of Christ.

If you can understand a people so long-suffering, so tolerant, so forgiving, so Christian after what they had suffered, you will have unlocked the key to what a Latter-day Saint is. Rather than being consumed with revenge, they were anchored to revelation. Their course was set by the teachings still found today in the Old and the New Testaments, the Book of Mormon, the Doctrine and Covenants, and the Pearl of Great Price.

If you can understand why they would celebrate as they did, you can understand why we have faith in the Lord Jesus Christ, in the principles of the gospel.

The Book of Mormon teaches, "We talk of Christ, we rejoice in Christ, we preach of Christ, we prophesy of Christ, and we write according to our prophecies, that our children may know to what source they may look for a remission of their sins" (2 Nephi 25:26).

And so today in these strangely perilous times, in the true Church of Jesus Christ we teach and live the principles of His gospel.

Three things about that 1849 commemoration were both symbolic and prophetic: first, that the young men carried the Constitution and the Declaration of Independence; next, that each young woman carried the Bible and the Book of Mormon; and finally, that the old men—the Silver Greys—were honored in the parade.

After the program they had a feast at makeshift tables. Several hundred gold-rush travelers and sixty Native Americans were invited to join them.

Then they went back to work.

President Young had said, "If the people of the United States will let us alone for ten years we will ask no odds of them" ("Remarks," *Deseret News,* Sept. 23, 1857, 228).

Eight years to the day after the 1849 celebration, the Saints were in Big Cottonwood Canyon to celebrate another 24th of July. Four horsemen rode in to report that an army 2,500 soldiers strong was on the plains. The army of the United States, commanded by Colonel Albert Sydney Johnston, was ordered by President James Buchanan to crush a nonexistent Mormon rebellion.

The Saints broke camp and headed for home to prepare their defenses. Rather than flee, this time President Young declared, "We have transgressed no law, and we have no occasion to do so, neither do we intend to; but as for any nation's coming to destroy this people, God Almighty being my helper, they cannot come here" ("Remarks," 228).

These events are a part of my own personal heritage. My great-grandparents buried a child on the trail from Far West when they were driven to Nauvoo, and another at Winter Quarters when they were driven west.

Another great-grandmother, a teenager, was pushing a handcart along the south banks of the Platte River. The members of her company sang:

> *We'll find the place which God for us prepared,*
> *Far away in the West,*
> *Where none shall come to hurt or make afraid;*
> *There the Saints will be blessed.*
> ("Come, Come, Ye Saints," *Hymns* [1985], no. 30)

Across the river they could see the sun glinting on the weapons of the soldiers of the army (see "By Handcart to Utah: The Account of C. C. A. Christensen," *Nebraska History,* Winter 1985, 342).

In St. Louis my great-grandmother bought a little enameled pin of the American flag. She wore it on her dress for the rest of her life.

Neither mobbings nor the army could turn the Saints aside

from what they knew to be true. A settlement was negotiated, and the Utah War (later called Buchanan's Blunder) was over.

We are guided by the same revelations as our ancestors, and we are led by a prophet, as they were. When the Prophet Joseph Smith died, another took his place. The order of succession continues today.

That same Lucifer who was cast out of our Father's presence is still at work. He, with the angels who followed him, will trouble the work of the Lord and destroy it if he can.

But we will stay on course. We will anchor ourselves as families and as a Church to these principles and ordinances. "The Standard of Truth has been erected; no unhallowed hand can stop the work from progressing" (Smith, *History of the Church,* 4:540).Whatever tests lie ahead, and they will be many, we must remain faithful and true.

CHAPTER 11

Truths Most
Worth Knowing

I have watched my senior Brethren move around the circle and then graduate to the other side of the veil—so many great ones. President Harold B. Lee told me that I should associate with the older Brethren and learn from their experiences. I followed that counsel. From Henry Wadsworth Longfellow:

> Lives of great men all remind us
> We can make our lives sublime,
> And, departing, leave behind us
> Footprints on the sands of time;
>
> Footprints, that perhaps another,
> Sailing o'er life's solemn main,

From a talk given at a Church Educational System devotional, November 6, 2011, Brigham Young University.

A forlorn and shipwrecked brother,
Seeing, shall take heart again.
("A Psalm of Life," in *The Complete*
Poetical Works of Longfellow [1883], 3)

These "footprints on the sands of time" will always remain visible to help guide you.

When I was a young member of the Quorum of the Twelve, we walked from our weekly temple meetings back to our offices. I would linger behind and walk with Elder LeGrand Richards. He had been somewhat crippled in an accident in his youth and walked more slowly than the others.

The other Brethren would say, "You are so kind to take care of Elder Richards," and I would answer, "You don't know why I do it!"

As we walked, I listened. He could remember President Wilford Woodruff. He was twelve years old the last time he heard President Woodruff speak. Elder Richards was a link to that generation. I absorbed every word he spoke.

There is a charge given to the Twelve in the Doctrine and Covenants: "The twelve traveling councilors are called to be the Twelve Apostles, or special witnesses of the name of Christ in all the world" (D&C 107:23).

I have had an unquenchable desire to bear testimony of the Father and of Jesus Christ. Christ said, "If ye had known me, ye should have known my Father also" (John 14:7). I have yearned to tell what I know about what Christ did and who the Father and the Son are.

I know words carried by the gift of the Holy Ghost can

bring to your understanding "the truth of all things" (Moroni 10:5). All truth is worth knowing. Some truths are more useful, but there are truths that are most worth knowing.

Experience Helps Us Understand Our Heavenly Father's Love for His Children

I have asked young missionaries, "Do you know what the word *father* means?" They say, of course, they do know. I respect their answer, but deep down I think, "You know so very little." They do know what the word *father* means, but their knowledge is immature.

To you who are married and have a child, the word *father* takes on a new meaning; the word *father* comes into clearer focus.

Perhaps there will come a day when a doctor tells you, "I think you are not going to keep this one." Finally, you learn about the Father and about yourself.

We had been married for nine years when we first heard those words from the doctor: "I'm afraid you're not going to keep this one." As parents, we looked at our tiny baby son and did the only thing we could do. He was named and given a father's blessing in the hospital. We prayed, had faith, and said aloud, "Thy will be done."

Hours passed, and then days. The doctors and nurses continued to work with our son.

At last we heard the words from the doctor, "I believe you *will* keep this one."

As parents, we grew in understanding and strength and drew closer to each other and to the Father.

Thirteen years later, in a much larger hospital, that experience was repeated with our tenth child. He was given a name and a father's blessing in the hospital. We prayed, had faith, and once again said aloud, "Thy will be done."

Hours crept slowly by. Once again we were greatly blessed. He would live. The lessons learned years before had been repeated.

One day you may find yourself in circumstances that cause you to know that you would give your life if your little one could live to experience mortality. You then can begin to understand our Heavenly Father. Then you will truly know what the words *father* and *mother* mean.

Many times I have yearned to relieve the suffering of a child or erase the grief or pain from someone that I love, only to realize that I could not do that. But I have learned that the fact that I would do it if I could is of very great consequence in my relationship to the Lord.

Our Need for a Mediator

There is a puzzle in the scriptures about justice and mercy. These are two seemingly conflicting principles that I addressed on another occasion by teaching somewhat of a parable (see "The Mediator," *Ensign*, May 1977, 54–56). The story goes like this:

There once was a man who wanted something very much. It seemed more important than anything else in his life. In order for him to have his desire, he incurred a great debt.

He had been warned about going into that much debt and

particularly about his creditor. But it seemed so important for him to do what he wanted to do and to have what he wanted right now. He was sure he could pay for it later. So he signed a contract with a lender. He would pay it off sometime along the way. He did not worry too much about it, for the due date seemed such a long time off. He had what he wanted now, and that was what seemed important.

The lender or creditor was always somewhere in the back of his mind, and he made token payments now and again, thinking somehow that the day of reckoning really would never come. But as it always does, the day came, and the contract fell due. The debt had not been paid.

His creditor appeared and demanded payment in full. Only then did he realize that his creditor not only had the power to repossess all that he owned, but the power to cast him into debtor's prison.

"I cannot pay you, for I have not the power to do so," he confessed.

"Then," said the creditor, "we will enforce the contract, take your possessions, and you shall go to prison. You agreed to that. It was your choice. You signed the contract, and now it must be enforced."

"Can you not show mercy? Can you not extend the time or forgive the debt?" the debtor begged. "Arrange some way for me to keep what I have and not go to prison. Will you not be merciful? Surely you believe in mercy?"

The creditor replied, "Mercy is always so one-sided. It would serve only you. If I show mercy to you, it will leave me unpaid. It is justice I demand. Do you believe in justice?"

"I believed in justice when I signed the contract," the debtor said. "It was on my side then, for I thought it would protect me. I did not need mercy then nor think I should ever need it. Justice, I thought, would serve both of us equally well."

"It is justice that demands that you pay the contract or suffer the penalty," the creditor replied. "That is the law. You have agreed to it, and that is the way it must be."

There they were: one meting out justice, the other pleading for mercy. Neither could prevail except at the expense of the other.

"If you do not forgive the debt, there will be no mercy," the debtor pleaded.

"If I do, there will be no justice," was the reply.

Both laws, it seemed, could not be served. Mercy cannot rob justice (see Alma 42:25). Each is an eternal ideal that appears to contradict the other. Is there no way for justice to be fully served and mercy also?

There is a way! The law of justice can be fully satisfied and mercy can be fully extended, but it takes someone else. And so it happened this time.

The debtor had a friend. He came to help. He knew the debtor well. He knew him to be shortsighted. He thought him foolish to have gotten himself into such a predicament. Nevertheless, he wanted to help because he loved him. He stepped between them as a mediator and made this offer to the creditor: "I will pay the debt if you will free the debtor from his contract so that he may keep his possessions and not go to prison."

As the creditor was pondering the offer, the mediator

added, "You demanded justice. Although he cannot pay you, I will do so. You will have been justly dealt with and can ask no more. That would not be just."

The mediator then turned to the debtor. "If I pay your debt, will you accept me as your creditor?"

"Oh, yes," cried the debtor. "You save me from prison and show mercy to me."

"Then," said the mediator, "you will pay the debt to me, and I will set the terms. It will not be easy, but it will be possible. I will provide a way. You need not go to prison."

And so it was that the creditor was paid in full. He had been justly dealt with. No contract had been broken. The debtor, in turn, had been extended mercy. Both laws stood fulfilled. Because there was a mediator, justice had claimed its full share and mercy was fully satisfied.

Unless there is a mediator, unless we have a friend, the full weight of justice, untempered and unsympathetic, must—positively must—fall on us. The full penalty for every transgression, however minor or however deep, will be exacted from us to the uttermost farthing.

There is a Mediator, a Redeemer who stands both willing and able to appease the demands of justice and extend mercy to those who are penitent, for "he offereth himself a sacrifice for sin, to answer the ends of the law, unto all those who have a broken heart and a contrite spirit; and unto none else can the ends of the law be answered" (2 Nephi 2:7). All will one day stand before Him "to be judged at the last . . . judgment day, according to their works" (Alma 33:22), "for there is one God,

If at first you stumble,

DO

NOT

GIVE

UP.

Overcoming discouragement

is part of the test.

DO NOT GIVE UP.

and one mediator between God and men, the man Christ Jesus" (1 Timothy 2:5).

Through Him, mercy can be fully extended to each of us without offending the eternal law of justice. The extension of mercy will not be automatic. It will come through covenant with Him. It will be on His terms—His generous terms.

To activate His mercy, we must repent. Our transgressions are all added to our account, and one day, if it is not properly settled, unless we have repented, each of us will be found wanting and stand condemned.

Repentance Erases Guilt and Disappointment

We all live on spiritual credit. In one way or another, the account builds and builds. If you pay it off as you go, you have little need to worry. Soon you begin to learn discipline and know that there is a day of reckoning ahead. Learn to keep your spiritual account paid off at regular intervals rather than allowing it to collect interest and penalties.

Because you are being tested, it is expected that you will make some mistakes. I assume that you have done things in your life that you regret, things that you cannot even apologize for, much less correct; therefore, you carry a burden. It is time now to use the word *guilt,* which can stain like indelible ink and cannot easily be washed away. A stepchild of guilt is disappointment, regret for lost blessings and opportunities.

If you are struggling with guilt, you are not unlike the people of the Book of Mormon of whom the prophet said, "Because of their iniquity the church had begun to dwindle;

and they began to disbelieve in the spirit of prophecy and in the spirit of revelation; and the judgments of God did stare them in the face" (Helaman 4:23).

We often try to solve the problem of guilt by telling one another and telling ourselves that it does not matter. But somehow, deep inside, we do not believe this. Nor do we believe ourselves if we say it. We know better. It does matter!

Prophets have always taught repentance. Alma said, "Behold, he cometh to redeem those who will be baptized unto repentance, through faith on his name" (Alma 9:27).

Alma bluntly told his wayward son, "Now, repentance could not come unto men except there were a punishment, which also was eternal as the life of the soul should be, affixed opposite to the plan of happiness" (Alma 42:16).

There are two basic purposes for mortal life. The first is to receive a body, which can, if we will, be purified and exalted and live forever. The second purpose is to be tested. In testing, we certainly will make mistakes. But if we will, we can learn from our mistakes. "If we say that we have not sinned, we make him a liar, and his word is not in us" (1 John 1:10).

You perhaps may feel inferior in mind and body, troubled or burdened with the weight of some spiritual account that is marked "past due." When you come face-to-face with yourself in those moments of quiet contemplation (which many of us try to avoid), are there some unsettled things that bother you? Do you have something on your conscience? Are you still, to one degree or another, guilty of anything small or large?

Too frequently we receive letters from those who have made

tragic mistakes and are burdened. They beg: "Can I ever be forgiven? Can I ever change?" The answer is yes!

Paul taught the Corinthians, "There hath no temptation taken you but such as is common to man: but God is faithful, who will not suffer you to be tempted above that ye are able; but will with the temptation also make a way to escape, that ye may be able to bear it" (1 Corinthians 10:13).

The gospel teaches us that relief from torment and guilt can be earned through repentance. Save for those few—those very few—who defect to perdition after having known a fulness, there is no habit, no addiction, no rebellion, no transgression, no offense small or large which is exempt from the promise of complete forgiveness. No matter what has happened in your life, the Lord has prepared a way for you to come back if you will heed the promptings of the Holy Spirit.

Some are filled with a compelling urge, a temptation that recycles in the mind, perhaps to become a habit, then an addiction. We are prone to some transgression and sin and also a rationalization that we have no guilt because we were born that way. We become trapped, and hence comes the pain and torment that only the Savior can heal. You have the power to stop and to be redeemed.

Satan Attacks the Family

President Marion G. Romney told me once, "Don't just tell them so that they can understand, tell them so that they cannot misunderstand."

Nephi said: "For my soul delighteth in plainness; for after

this manner doth the Lord God work among the children of men. For the Lord God giveth light unto the understanding" (2 Nephi 31:3).

So I will speak plainly as one called and under obligation to do so.

You know that there is an adversary. The scriptures define him in these terms: "That old serpent, who is the devil, . . . the father of all lies" (2 Nephi 2:18). He was cast out in the beginning (see D&C 29:36–38) and denied a mortal body. He has now sworn to disrupt "the great plan of happiness" (Alma 42:8) and become an enemy to all righteousness. He focuses his attacks on the family.

You live in a day when the scourge of pornography is sweeping across the world. It is hard to escape it. Pornography is focused on that part of your nature through which you have the power to beget life.

To indulge in pornography leads to difficulties, divorce, disease, and troubles of a dozen kinds. There is no part of it that is innocent. To collect it, view it, or carry it around in any form is akin to keeping a rattlesnake in your backpack. It exposes you to the inevitable spiritual equivalent of the serpent's strike with its injection of deadly venom. One can easily understand, with the world being what it is, that you can almost innocently be exposed to it, to read it, or to view it without realizing the terrible consequences. If that describes you, I warn you to stop it. Stop it now!

The Book of Mormon teaches that all "men are instructed sufficiently that they know good from evil" (2 Nephi 2:5).

That includes you. You know what is right and what is wrong. Be very careful not to cross that line.

Although most mistakes can be confessed privately to the Lord, there are some transgressions that require more than that to bring about forgiveness. If your mistakes have been grievous, see your bishop. Otherwise, ordinary confession, quietly and personally, will do. But remember, that great morning of forgiveness may not come all at once. If at first you stumble, do not give up. Overcoming discouragement is part of the test. Do not give up. And as I have counseled before, once you have confessed and forsaken your sins, do not look back.

The Lord is always there. He has suffered and paid the penalty if you are willing to accept Him as your Redeemer.

The Savior's Suffering Was for Our Sins

As mortals, we may not, indeed cannot, understand fully *how* He fulfilled His atoning sacrifice. But for now the *how* is not as important as the *why* of His suffering. Why did He do it for you, for me, for all of humanity? He did it for the love of God the Father and all mankind. "Greater love hath no man than this, that a man lay down his life for his friends" (John 15:13).

In Gethsemane, Christ went apart from His Apostles to pray. Whatever transpired is beyond our power to know! But we do know that He completed the Atonement. He was willing to take upon Himself the mistakes, the sins and guilt, the doubts and fears of all the world. He suffered for us so that we would not have to suffer. Many mortals have suffered torment and died a painful, terrible death. But His agony surpassed them all.

At my age, I have come to know what physical pain is, and it is no fun! Nobody escapes this life without learning a thing or two about suffering. But the personal torment that I cannot bear is when I have come to know that I have caused another to suffer. It is then that I catch a glimpse of the agony the Savior experienced in the Garden of Gethsemane.

His suffering was different than all others before or since had experienced because He took upon Himself all of the penalties that had ever been imposed on the human family. Imagine that! He had no debt to pay. He had committed no wrong. Nevertheless, an accumulation of all of the guilt, the grief and sorrow, the pain and humiliation, all of the mental, emotional, and physical torments known to man—He experienced them all. There has been only One in all the annals of human history who was entirely sinless, qualified to answer for the sins and transgressions of all mankind and survive the pain that accompanied paying for them.

He presented His life and in essence said, "It is I that taketh upon me the sins of the world" (Mosiah 26:23). He was crucified; He died. They could not take His life from Him. He consented to die.

Complete Forgiveness Is Possible

If you have stumbled or even been lost for a time, if you feel that the adversary now holds you captive, you can move forward with faith and not wander to and fro in the world any longer. There are those who stand ready to guide you back to peace and security. Even the grace of God, as promised in the scriptures, comes "after all we can do" (2 Nephi 25:23). The possibility of this, to me, is the truth most worth knowing.

I promise that the brilliant morning of forgiveness can come. Then "the peace of God, which passeth all understanding" (Philippians 4:7) comes into your life once again, something like a sunrise, and you and He "will remember [your] sin no more" (Jeremiah 31:34). How will you know? You will know! (see Mosiah 4:1–3).

This is what I wish to teach you who are in trouble. He will step in and solve the problem you cannot solve, but you have to pay the price. It does not come without doing that. He is a very kind ruler in the sense that He has paid the price necessary, but He wants you to do what you should, even if it is painful.

I love the Lord, and I love the Father who sent Him. Our burdens of disappointment, sin, and guilt can be laid before Him, and on His generous terms, each item on the account can be marked "paid in full."

CHAPTER 12

The Foundation of
Your Character

When I was five years old I became very ill. It later turned out that I had polio. That was not diagnosed by the small-town doctor. I lay for several weeks on a World War I army cot in our front room beside a coal stove. After those weeks, the doctor said I could get up, having been cured of "pneumonia." I found I could not walk. I remember clearly sliding around on the linoleum floor and pulling myself up on the chairs and learning to walk again.

As I moved on into elementary school and junior high and then into high school, I found that my muscles were very weak. I was very self-conscious. I could not be an athlete.

And it did not help a lot when I read about the man who went to a doctor to see if he could get some help with his

From a talk given at a Church Educational System fireside, February 2, 2003, Brigham Young University.

inferiority complex. The doctor studied him for a while and said, "You don't have a complex. You *are* inferior!"

With that encouragement, I set about through life and tried to compensate in other ways.

Just as we were about to graduate from high school, World War II opened up. As senior boys, we all lamented that the war would be over before we were out of high school in June. Little did we know!

My older brother was a pilot, and I thought, "Well, I am going to be drafted. I think I will at least try to enlist in the Air Cadet pilot training program." To my surprise, I passed the physical. In looking back on that, I can see two reasons for it: one was that they had learned that you did not have to be a well-muscled athlete to fly a plane. The other reason was perhaps more important: they needed tens of thousands of pilots and bombardiers and navigators.

And so I went to basic training—boot camp—and there the physical training was very rigorous.

I soon found myself in the Air Cadet program, where the physical part of it was also very strenuous. So I was back on the army cot, lying at night in agony with aching muscles and swollen limbs and the thought that in the morning we would go right at it again. Actually, that was the best possible therapy.

In that time, I learned to pray. I learned the difference between saying prayers and praying, earnestly praying for health and strength and wisdom.

And then something happened that changed my life entirely in a remarkable way. I had my patriarchal blessing. Usually these are very, very private, and we do not talk about them or read them with others. But I am going to share a paragraph or two with you here. The patriarch, whom I had never met before, blessed me in this way, in part:

"You had the opportunity before coming here to voice your desire to have this privilege of Earth Life in the council of the spirit world. You were valiant in the defense of truth and right. You made a free and willing decision to abide by the laws of Eternal Progress as outlined by our elder brother, the Lord Jesus Christ. You kept faithfully your first estate and have been added upon by being born into this world and given a physical body with which you might experience Earth Life. You have been given a body of such physical proportions and fitness as to enable your spirit to function through it unhampered by physical impediments. You should cherish this as a great heritage. Guard and protect it—take nothing into it that shall harm the organs thereof because it is sacred. It is the instrument of your mind and the foundation of your character" (patriarchal blessing of Boyd K. Packer, January 15, 1944, 1).

All at once, I did not care what kind of a body I had. I had a body of sufficient capacity to let my spirit function through it. I had learned that a body is sacred.

I found that it did not matter, really, what kind of bodies we have, so long as we understand that our spirit and our body are combined in such a way that our body becomes an instrument of our mind and the foundation of our character.

From then on, I saw no purpose, nothing to be gained, by talking to other people about my aches and pains. I just moved on through life.

Joseph Smith taught: "We came to this earth that we might

have a body and present it pure before God in the celestial kingdom. The great principle of happiness consists in having a body. The devil has no body, and herein is his punishment. . . . All beings who have bodies have power over those who have not. The devil has no power over us only as we permit him. The moment we revolt at anything which comes from God, the devil takes power" (*Teachings of the Prophet Joseph Smith,* sel. Joseph Fielding Smith [1976], 181).

Now, let me restate that: The punishment of the adversary was that he did not receive a body. All beings who have bodies, as the Prophet said, will have power over those who do not. The devil has no power over us, only as we permit him.

That was a great moment of enlightenment when I read in my patriarchal blessing. And then, as I began to study and learn, there came the knowledge and understanding of who we are and where we came from.

I was in the military—had not been on a mission, had not had any college, and often was alone. We often are alone, all of us, in our lives. I became a product of the Book of Mormon.

Knowledge of Right and Wrong

From the Book of Mormon I learned something that is very important. Mormon taught: "For behold, the Spirit of Christ is given to every man, that he may know good from evil; wherefore, I show unto you the way to judge; for every thing which inviteth to do good, and to persuade to believe in Christ, is sent forth by the power and gift of Christ; wherefore ye may know with a perfect knowledge it is of God" (Moroni 7:16).

I had already read, when I came to that, the statement of Nephi in 2 Nephi that all "men are instructed sufficiently that they know good from evil" (2 Nephi 2:5).

So that is built into us. We know what is right and what is wrong. We all know. That is a very important thing to understand. As we move through life, we begin to understand some other things.

We live in very troubled times—the beginning of even more troubled times. What we faced in World War II, the jeopardy and challenge, was nothing compared to what young people face now. It is a terrible and challenging time and, at once, perhaps the best time ever in the history of mankind to be alive.

I want to make this point: In the premortal existence, we were given spirit bodies, and we were given agency. So we are free. In the Doctrine and Covenants we read:

"And no man receiveth a fulness unless he keepeth his commandments.

"He that keepeth his commandments receiveth truth and light, until he is glorified in truth and knoweth all things.

"Man was also in the beginning with God. Intelligence, or the light of truth, was not created or made, neither indeed can be.

"All truth is independent in that sphere in which God has placed it, to act for itself" (D&C 93:27–30).

So there we are. We have agency. What happens in our

lives and in our pattern of eternal progression is just what we decide it will be.

"All truth is independent in that sphere in which God has placed it, to act for itself, as all intelligence also; otherwise there is no existence.

"Behold, here is the agency of man" (D&C 93:30–31).

The Great Plan of Redemption and the Word of Wisdom

As we learn about ourselves and learn about the great plan of redemption, we know that in the premortal existence intelligence existed forever. It was not created. It will exist forever. In due course, we were given a spirit body (see Acts 17:29; D&C 93:33–35; Abraham 3:22–23; 5:7). We became then the sons and daughters of God. We had gender then. We were male or female (see Genesis 1:27; Matthew 19:4; Mark 10:6; D&C 20:17–18; 132:63; Moses 2:27; 6:9; Abraham 4:27). While in that existence, we were valiant and chose good, as Alma recorded (see Alma 13:3).

Alma said that "God gave unto them commandments, *after* having made known unto them the plan of redemption" (Alma 12:32; emphasis added).

The great plan is called the great plan of redemption and six or seven other titles (see 2 Nephi 11:5; Alma 12:25; 17:16; 34:9; 41:2; 42:5, 11–13, 15, 31; D&C 101:22; Moses 6:62). Alma called it "the great plan of happiness" (Alma 42:8).

Then, in the course of our having chosen good, we had a body prepared by mortal parents, and we were born into mortality. With that came the power to create life, to follow the

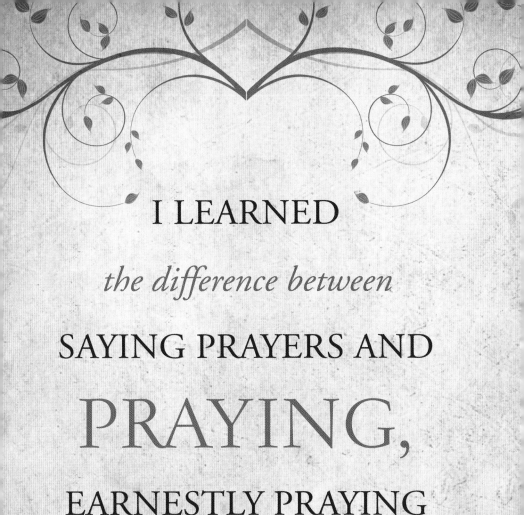

I LEARNED

the difference between

SAYING PRAYERS AND

PRAYING,

EARNESTLY PRAYING

for health and strength

and wisdom.

plan of redemption, the plan of happiness. How we employ that power and understand the supernal value of it is one major factor that will determine where we go in life.

That paragraph from my patriarchal blessing was a revelation to me. The patriarch, who is a prophet, said, "Take nothing into [the body that would] harm the organs thereof."

As I read the scriptures, I came to section 89 and learned that it was "a Word of Wisdom, . . . given for a principle with promise, adapted to the capacity of the weak and the weakest of all saints, who are or can be called saints" (D&C 89:1, 3). And "the weakest of all saints" included me.

There was another essential point. The Lord said, "In consequence of evils and designs which do and will exist in the hearts of conspiring men in the last days, I have warned you, and forewarn you, by giving unto you this word of wisdom by revelation" (D&C 89:4).

The scriptures say elsewhere that "this is a day of warning, and not a day of many words" (D&C 63:58).

The "Word of Wisdom [was] given for a principle with promise" (D&C 89:1, 3). But what is the promise? The promise, of course, is personal revelation.

"[Those who remember to do these things will] receive health in their navel and marrow to their bones; . . .

"And shall run and not be weary, and shall walk and not faint. [And that means we will have some measure of health, which, I have learned, is of secondary importance.]

"And I, the Lord, give unto them a promise, that the destroying angel shall pass by them, as the children of Israel, and not slay them" (D&C 89:18, 20–21).

And this: "[You shall receive] great treasures of knowledge, even hidden treasures" (D&C 89:19).

Now, the Word of Wisdom is, I think, only incidentally to keep us healthy, if we will observe it. But that matter of physical health is a losing battle. You know, no matter what you do to take care of your body, in due course, it begins to weaken! We are not going to live forever in this life. We can live with our infirmities.

I remember once we were having a sacrament meeting in the temple. Elder Marion D. Hanks was passing the sacrament. I had a catch in my shoulder, and I could not get my hand up to the bread plate. It was very awkward. I was very embarrassed. Finally, we accomplished it, and later I apologized to him and said, "I just couldn't; my shoulder just wouldn't move!"

And he said, "My shoulder wouldn't move, either! I couldn't get the thing down to you!" So that was some comfort.

We have accepted as the Word of Wisdom in the Church standards that we will not change. You are not going to go on a mission unless you observe it. You are not going to go to the temple for the more sacred ordinances unless you observe it.

We get strange letters asking if this or that is a part of the Word of Wisdom. Marijuana is not listed in section 89. And neither is strychnine or arsenic listed! But, of course, those are not habit-forming.

The point is, if you want to move on spiritually and do as you ought to do in this life, the principle outlined in the Word of Wisdom shows you the requirements. You cannot just toy with it.

One day, before a seminary class began, some students were standing at the back of the room. It was a Monday. A new girl in the class overheard them. These very foolish young people were talking about their weekend and what drinks they had. One of them turned to her and said, "What is your favorite drink?"

She said, "Water, stupid!"

And so, like it or not, if you are tampering, if there is any mischief, you have got to quit it! It is not that you are going to be a healthy athlete all your life, and it is not that you are going to avoid old age. It is that you *will* have the key to revelation. When your body begins to deteriorate, the patterns of revelation will be augmented and magnified.

Two Conflicting Influences

Another important thing to remember is that the Holy Ghost is conferred upon us at the time of baptism. Remember, "first, Faith in the Lord Jesus Christ; second, Repentance; third, Baptism by immersion for the remission of sins; fourth, Laying on of hands for the gift of the Holy Ghost" (Articles of Faith 1:4).

In the Book of Mormon again: "Angels speak by the power of the Holy Ghost; wherefore, they speak the words of Christ. Wherefore, I said unto you, feast upon the words of Christ; for behold, the words of Christ will tell you all things what ye should do" (2 Nephi 32:3).

If you will keep your body in a worthy, receptive circumstance, you will be prompted, even have angels attend you.

Angels will attend you and will "speak [to you] by the power of the Holy Ghost."

But you also should know, as Moroni said, "[The devil] persuadeth no man to do good, no, not one; neither do his angels; neither do they who subject themselves unto him" (Moroni 7:17).

So you are the focus of two conflicting patterns trying to influence you in your life, trying to have you go this way or that way (see Matthew 6:24; Luke 16:13; James 1:8). You are the one who makes the decision.

As a wise old man a generation ago said, "The Lord's votin' for me, and the devil's votin' against me, but it's my vote that counts!" And that is good, solid doctrine.

You will have just what you want. On one hand, you have inspiration from the Holy Ghost, and, on the other hand, you have what President Ezra Taft Benson called "sinspiration" from the angels of the devil. They are with you all the time.

I gave a talk once in which I likened the mind to a stage. There is always something going on in that stage. Whatever you think is going on in the stage, these ideas and promptings and temptations will move in from the side. What do you do about it? You ought to have a delete key.

I know a little about computers because my grandchildren have taught me. I know that every computer keyboard has a delete key. If there is something in your document that you do not want, something you did that you want to get rid of, you highlight it and delete it.

You can have a delete key in your mind. Your mind is in

charge, and your body is the instrument of your mind. Now you will have to figure out a delete key for yourself.

One man showed me once that he used his wedding ring. He said that whenever there was an unworthy thought that tried to get into his mind—and those influences are everywhere—he just rubbed his thumb against his wedding ring. That was the delete key, "Get out of my mind! I am in charge!"

You are in command. You cannot say that you do not know any better. You do know better!

There are other ways to push a delete key for unwelcome thoughts. Music is powerful. My older brother taught me that.

When he was flying in the Eighth Air Force, it was terrible. He was shot down twice. But he said finally he got so he was not afraid. He was not afraid because when fear came, he turned on this little orchestra in his mind. He took his favorite hymn and played it over and over in his mind.

I learned something, and I have since lived that way. When some ugly thought from the nether kingdom tries to get into my mind, I move it out with good music, with hymns (see D&C 25:12).

That is one of the reasons why it is so very foolish to participate in music that is dark and noisy: Worthy inspiration cannot get through to you where you are. No matter how popular such things may be or how much you want to belong, just remember that there are those angels of the devil using you.

Remember the incident when Christ crossed the water and came to a cave where there were two wild men possessed of the devils. Those spirits said to Him, "What have we to do with [you]?" (Matthew 8:29). They knew what was going to happen.

They begged, "If thou cast us out, suffer us to go away into the herd of swine" (Matthew 8:31). There was a herd of swine feeding there. They would rather go there. They did not have a body, could not get a body, would not ever have a body, and they were temporarily in possession of the bodies of those poor men. Christ did that. Then it records that the swine ran away into the sea and were drowned (see Matthew 8:28–32).

Learn from the scriptures. They are teaching you—teaching about everyday life.

Marriage and the Sacred Powers of Creation

Two decades ago, the First Presidency and Quorum of the Twelve issued a proclamation on the family. I can tell you how that came about. There was a world conference on the family sponsored by the United Nations in Beijing, China. We sent representatives. What they heard was not pleasant. I read the proceedings of that conference. The word *marriage* was not mentioned. It was a conference on the family, but marriage was not even mentioned.

Then the announcement came that they were going to have such a conference here in Salt Lake City. Some of us made the recommendation: "They are coming here. We had better proclaim our position."

You read the proclamation on the family. Read it carefully. This is the first paragraph:

"We, the First Presidency and the Council of the Twelve

Apostles of The Church of Jesus Christ of Latter-day Saints, solemnly proclaim that marriage between a man and a woman is ordained of God and that the family is central to the Creator's plan for the eternal destiny of His children" ("The Family: A Proclamation to the World," *Ensign,* Nov. 1995, 102).

Here the physical body comes into play. Within us is the sacred power of creation. The adversary is busy with all his angels focusing right to the bull's-eye of what would destroy us quickest.

There is the matter of pornography. It has become almost a pornographic world. Now, you leave it alone! If you have any, destroy it! And if you know somebody that has it, help them destroy it! And do not look at it, not ever! It is destructive, and it will take you on a path that is not consistent with who you are and what you can decide. Do not watch it, not ever!

To talk in something less than casual terms, do not ever let anybody touch your body in order to stimulate in any way those sacred powers of creation. Nobody! Not of your same gender or any gender! That power is to be expressed only and solely with your husband or wife to whom you are legally and lawfully married (see D&C 42:22). Then all of the happiness possible is open to you. You must guard that sacred power with your life.

If you young women are going with a young man who wants to take you to places where you should not go, however appealing, to those dark and noisy places, and there is some move to try to get you to do something you know you should not do, cut it off. Break it up! Send him a letter. Stamp it "Second-Class Male."

It is just that serious. No pornography! No mischief! You save those creative powers until they are used for the purpose for which they were intended: to create a family.

There are natural instincts, and they are very strong; they have to be. And they are good! There are also cravings and temptations. There can be habitual self-stimulation and a lot of things that are just unworthy of you.

The young men are not the only ones. We are finding now that the young women, unaccustomed in times past, are becoming aggressive. You young men guard yourselves. You just let it be known that you have ahead of you the fulfillment of the blessings that come with the great plan of happiness. There is not a man that I know who cannot send a woman who has those designs away with just a look or a gesture and just *No!* And the same with those young women to those young men.

You may feel alone. A lot of times you are alone. But that is part of what life is.

Fixing What Is Broken

Over the years, as a diversion, I have carved wooden birds. Sometimes it would take a year to complete one. I would get specimens and measure the feathers and study the colors and then carve them. I would carve a setting for them. It was very restful. Sometimes when I would get unsettled, my wife would say, "Why don't you go carve a bird!" It was a very calming thing in my life.

Elder A. Theodore Tuttle and I were going into town one day. I had one of the carvings. I was taking it in to show someone. We had put it on the backseat. At an intersection, he slammed on the brakes, and the carving tipped upside down on the floor and broke to pieces. He pulled over to the side and looked at it. He was devastated. I was not.

Without thinking, I said, "Forget it. I made it. I can fix it." And I did. I made it stronger than it was. I improved it a bit.

Now, who made you? Who is your Creator? There is not anything about your life that gets bent or broken that He cannot fix and will fix. You have to decide. If you have made mistakes and you think you are broken and cannot be put together, you do not know the doctrine of the Church. You do not know what the Atonement was about and who the Lord is and what a power He is in your life.

This is His Church. We are His servants. We who hold the priesthood have His authority and power. We can perform miracles. We do not talk about them. Many of those miracles have to do with healing the body. The greater miracles are the miracles of spiritual growth and healing in the lives of every one of us.

So if you are on the wrong path, then you must decide. You have the agency. You have the promptings of the Holy Ghost to guide you. There is that great truth that the gospel is a gospel of repentance. Repentance is like a mathematical equation. Repentance leads to forgiveness.

A Marvelous Time to Be Alive

It is a marvelous time to be alive. The world is not going to come to an end anytime soon. You are going to have time to stand, as I stand now, talking about your children and your grandchildren and your great-grandchildren. You decide!

You were born as spirit children of God in the premortal existence. You were born to earthly parents in this life. "The spirit and the body [eternally combined, the Lord said,] receive a fulness of joy" (D&C 138:17; see also D&C 93:33–34). "And the spirit and the body [combined] are the soul of man" (D&C 88:15).

You are consummately precious to the Lord, to the Church, to your parents, to one another. You now must decide what is right—you know what is right—and then have the courage to do it. You will be blessed and redeemed and exalted.

I bear witness that Jesus is the Christ. He lives. We know Him. He directs this Church. The gospel is true. The plan is a great plan of happiness. May you look forward to a marvelous life in the greatest work that has ever been on the face of this earth.

---○◦○---

CHAPTER 13

Lehi's Dream and You

My college life began at Weber College in Ogden, Utah, which was at that time a very small junior college. World War II had just ended. Most of the men in our class were recently returned from military service. We were, by and large, more mature than college students of today. We had been through the war and carried with us many memories. Some of them we held onto; others we were glad to have fade away. We wanted to get on with our lives and knew that education was the key.

We took the insignias and labels and sometimes even the buttons off our uniforms, mixed them with odds and ends of civilian clothes, and wore them to school. That was all we had to wear.

At military training camps, we had been marched from

From a talk given at a Brigham Young University devotional, January 16, 2007. See also Ensign, *August 2010, 20–25.*

place to place in formation. Often we would sing marching songs. At college, I attended the institute of religion classes. We had our own marching songs. I remember one of them:

A root-tee-toot, a root-tee-toot.
Oh, we are boys of the institute.
We don't smoke, and we don't chew.
And we don't go with girls that do.
Some folks say we don't have fun.
We don't!

Some laughed with us; others laughed at us. Whatever ridicule they intended with their mocking was of no concern to us. We had gained personal testimonies of the gospel. We had decided long since that we would live the gospel and not be ashamed of the Church or the history or any part of it (see Romans 1:16).

I did not serve a mission during those years. Staying close to the Book of Mormon has, I think, made up for that. That witness came little by little.

The whole focus of our lives in the military had been on destruction. That is what war is about. We were inspired by the noble virtue of patriotism. To be devoted to destruction without being destroyed yourself spiritually or morally was the test of life.

You too live in a time of war, the spiritual war that will never end. War itself now dominates the affairs of mankind. Your world at war has lost its innocence. There is nothing, however crude or unworthy, that is not deemed acceptable for movies or plays or music or conversation. The world seems to be turned upside down (see 2 Peter 2:1–22).

Formality, respect for authority, dignity, and nobility are mocked. Modesty and neatness yield to slouchiness and shabbiness in dress and grooming. The rules of honesty and integrity and basic morality are now ignored. Conversation is laced with profanity. You see that in art and literature, in drama and entertainment. Instead of being refined, they become coarse (see 1 Timothy 4:1–3; 2 Timothy 3:1–9).

You have decisions to make almost every day as to whether you will follow those trends. You have many tests ahead.

As a boy, President Joseph F. Smith, son of Hyrum, came west in 1848 with his widowed mother. He was called as a missionary to Hawaii when he was just fifteen years of age. He spent much of the next four years alone. He was released in 1857 at the age of nineteen. Penniless, he stopped in California to earn money for warm clothes.

"With another man, . . . [Joseph] took passage in a mail wagon. They traveled all night, and at daylight stopped near a ranch for breakfast. The passenger and the mail carrier began to prepare breakfast, while Joseph went a short distance from camp to [gather wood and] look after the horses. . . . A wagon load of drunken men from Monte came in view, on their road to San Bernardino to kill the 'Mormons,' as they boasted.

"The oaths and foul language which they uttered, between their shooting, and the swinging of their pistols, were almost indescribable. . . . They were all cursing the 'Mormons,' and uttering boasts of what they would do when they met them. They . . . caught sight of the mail wagon. . . . [His companion] and the mail carrier, fearing for their safety, had retired behind the chaparral, leaving all the baggage and supplies . . . exposed and unprotected.

"Just as [one] drunken man approached, [young Joseph F.] came in view . . . , too late to hide. . . . The ruffian was swinging his weapon, and uttering the most blood-curdling oaths and threats ever heard against the 'Mormons.' 'I dared not run,' says [Joseph F.] Smith, 'though I trembled for fear which I dared not show. I therefore walked right up to the camp fire, and arrived there just a minute or two before the drunken desperado, who came directly toward me, and, swinging his revolver in my face, with an oath cried out: "Are you a ___ ___ ___ 'Mormon?'"'"

"[Young Joseph] looked him straight in the eyes, and answered with emphasis: 'Yes, siree; dyed in the wool; true blue, through and through.'

"The desperado's arms both dropped by his sides, as if paralyzed, his pistol in one hand, and he said in a subdued . . . voice, offering his hand: 'Well, you are the ___ ___ pleasantest man I ever met! Shake. I am glad to see a fellow stand for his convictions.' Then he turned and [left]" (Joseph F. Smith, *Gospel Doctrine: Sermons and Writings of Joseph F. Smith* [1986], 531–32).

You will probably not face the kind of test that Joseph F. Smith faced. In ways, your tests are going to be harder.

In the eighth chapter of 1 Nephi, we read about Lehi's dream. He told his family, "Behold, I have dreamed a dream; or, in other words, I have seen a vision" (1 Nephi 8:2).

You may think that Lehi's dream or vision has no special

meaning for you, but it does. You are in it; all of us are in it. Nephi said, "[All scripture is likened] unto us, that it might be for our profit and learning" (1 Nephi 19:23).

Lehi's dream or vision of the iron rod has in it everything a Latter-day Saint needs to understand the test of life.

Lehi saw:

• A great and spacious building (see 1 Nephi 11:35–36; 12:18),
• A path following a river (see 1 Nephi 8:19–22),
• A mist of darkness (see 1 Nephi 12:16–17),
• An iron rod that led through the mist of darkness (see 1 Nephi 11:24–25),
• The tree of life, "whose fruit was desirable to make one happy" (1 Nephi 8:10; see also 1 Nephi 11:8–9, 21–24).

Read the account of this dream carefully; then read it again.

Lehi's son Nephi wrote: "I, Nephi, was desirous also that I might see, and hear, and know of these things, by the power of the Holy Ghost, which is the gift of God unto all those who diligently seek him. . . .

"For he that diligently seeketh shall find; and the mysteries of God shall be unfolded unto them, by the power of the Holy Ghost, as well in these times as in times of old, and as well in times of old as in times to come; wherefore, the course of the Lord is one eternal round" (1 Nephi 10:17, 19).

All of the symbolism in Lehi's dream was explained to his son Nephi, and Nephi wrote about it.

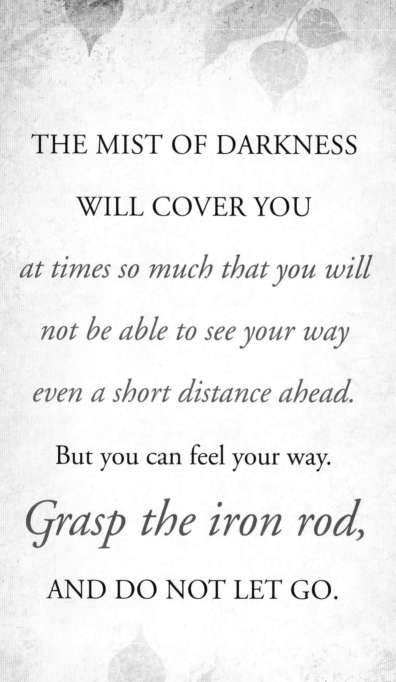

THE MIST OF DARKNESS

WILL COVER YOU

at times so much that you will

not be able to see your way

even a short distance ahead.

But you can feel your way.

Grasp the iron rod,

AND DO NOT LET GO.

Embedded in that dream or vision is the "pearl of great price" (Matthew 13:46). Lehi and Nephi saw:

- A virgin bearing a child in her arms,
- One who should prepare the way—John the Baptist,
- The ministry of the Son of God,
- Twelve others following the Messiah,
- The heavens open and angels ministering to them,
- The multitudes blessed and healed,
- And the Crucifixion of the Christ.

All of this they saw in dream or vision. And they saw the wisdom and pride of the world opposing His work (see 1 Nephi 11:14–36; see also 1 Nephi 1:9–14).

And that is what we face now.

Lehi saw great multitudes of people "pressing forward" (1 Nephi 8:21) toward the tree.

The great and spacious building "was filled with people, both old and young, both male and female; and their manner of dress was exceedingly fine; and they were in the attitude of mocking and pointing their fingers towards those who had come at and were partaking of the fruit" (1 Nephi 8:27).

One word in this dream or vision should have special meaning to us as Latter-day Saints. The word is *after*. It was *after* the people had found the tree that they became ashamed, and because of the mockery of the world they fell away.

"And *after* they had tasted of the fruit they were ashamed, because of those that were scoffing at them; and they fell away into forbidden paths and were lost. . . .

"And great was the multitude that did enter into that

strange building. And *after* they did enter into that building they did point the finger of scorn at me and those that were partaking of the fruit also"—that was the test, and then Lehi said—"but we heeded them not"—and that was the answer (1 Nephi 8:28, 33; italics added).

At your baptism and confirmation, you took hold of the iron rod. But you are never safe. It is *after* you have partaken of that fruit that your test will come.

I think now and then of one of our classmates—very bright, good-looking, faithful in the Church, and drenched with talent and ability. He married well and rose quickly to prominence. He began to compromise to please the world and please those around him. They flattered him into following after their ways, which were the ways of the world.

Somewhere, in little things, my classmate's grasp on the iron rod loosened a bit. His wife held on to the rod with one hand and to him with the other. Finally, he slipped away from her and let go of the rod. Just as Lehi's dream or vision predicted, he fell away into forbidden paths and was lost.

If you hold to the rod, you can *feel* your way forward with the gift of the Holy Ghost, which was conferred upon you at the time you were confirmed a member of the Church. The Holy Ghost will comfort you. You will be able to feel the influence of the angels, as Nephi did, and feel your way through life.

You will be safe if you look like and groom like and act like an ordinary Latter-day Saint: dress modestly, attend your meetings, pay tithes, take the sacrament, honor the priesthood, honor your parents, follow your leaders, read the scriptures, study the Book of Mormon, and pray, always pray. An unseen power will hold your hand as you hold to the iron rod.

Will this solve all your problems? Of course not! That would be contrary to the purpose of your coming into mortality. It will, however, give you a solid foundation on which to build your life (see Helaman 5:12).

The mist of darkness will cover you at times so much that you will not be able to see your way even a short distance ahead. You will not be able to see clearly. But you can *feel* your way. Grasp the iron rod, and do not let go. Through the power of the Holy Ghost, you can *feel* your way through life (see 3 Nephi 18:25; D&C 9:8).

We live in a time of war, that spiritual war that will never end. Moroni warned us that the secret combinations begun by Gadianton "are had among all people. . . .

"Wherefore, O ye Gentiles"—and the term *Gentile* in that place in the Book of Mormon refers to us in our generation—"it is wisdom in God that these things should be shown unto you, that thereby ye may repent of your sins, and suffer not that these murderous combinations shall get above you. . . .

"Wherefore, the Lord commandeth you, when ye shall see these things come among you that ye shall awake to a sense of your awful situation, because of this secret combination which shall be among you" (Ether 8:20, 23–24).

Atheists and agnostics make nonbelief their religion and today organize in unprecedented ways to attack faith and belief. They are now organized, and they pursue political power. You will be hearing much about them and from them. The types of Sherem, Nehor, and Korihor live among us today (see

Jacob 7:1–21; Alma 1:1–15; Alma 30:6–60). Their arguments are not so different from those in the Book of Mormon. Much of their attack is indirect in mocking the faithful, in mocking religion.

But all of the mocking does not come from outside of the Church. Let me repeat that: *All of the mocking does not come from outside of the Church.* Be careful that you do not fall into the category of mocking.

Even Moroni faced the same challenge. He said that because of his weakness in writing, "I fear . . . the Gentiles shall mock at our words."

And the Lord said to him: "Fools mock, but they shall mourn; and my grace is sufficient for the meek, that they shall take no advantage of your weakness;

"And if men come unto me I will show unto them their weakness. I give unto men weakness that they may be humble; and my grace is sufficient for all men that humble themselves before me; for if they humble themselves before me, and have faith in me, then will I make weak things become strong unto them" (Ether 12:25–27).

You live in an interesting generation when trials will be constant in your life. Learn to follow the promptings of the Holy Ghost. It is to be a shield and a protection and a teacher for you. Never be ashamed or embarrassed about the doctrines of the gospel or about the standards that we teach in the Church. You always, if you are faithful in the Church, will be that much different from the world at large. You have the advantage of being assured that you can be inspired in all of your decisions.

All of the things that you need to know are in the Book of Mormon, which can be your iron rod as it has always been mine. Read it, and make it a part of your life. Then the criticism or mocking of the world, the mocking of those in the Church, will be of no concern to you as it is of no concern to us as Church leaders (see 1 Nephi 8:33). We just move forward doing the things that we are called to do and know that the Lord is guiding us.

I pray the blessings of the Lord upon you in your work. I pray the blessings of the Lord upon you as you move forward from the morning of your life to the late evening, where I am now—that you will know that the gospel of Jesus Christ is true.

———◦◦◦———

CHAPTER 14

How to Survive in Enemy Territory

I wish to address these remarks to the youth of the Church. I write as one who has seen the past and would prepare you for the future. I want to tell you that which will be of most worth and most desirable. The scriptures say, "Wisdom is the principal thing; therefore get wisdom," and I would add, "with all [your] getting, get [going!]" (Proverbs 4:7). I do not have time to waste and neither do you.

Our Present Blessings Come from Past Sacrifices

The moment I decided to be a teacher is very clear in my mind. During World War II, I was in my early twenties and a pilot in the air force. I was stationed on the little island of Ie Shima. This island, a small, lonely one about as big as a postage stamp, is just off the northern tip of Okinawa.

From a talk given at a fireside commemorating 100 years of seminary, January 22, 2012.

One lonely summer evening I sat on a cliff to watch the sun go down. I remember looking at the moon and thinking, "That is the very same moon that shines down on my home in Utah." I was pondering what I would do with my life after the war, if I was fortunate enough to survive. What did I want to be? It was on that night that I decided I wanted to be a teacher. I reasoned that teachers are always learning. Learning is a basic purpose of life.

I first taught seminary in 1949 in Brigham City. I had been a student in that seminary in my high school days. There were three of us as teachers: the principal, Abel S. Rich, Brother A. Theodore Tuttle, and myself. Brother Rich had opened that seminary as the second released-time seminary in the Church. The first was established in 1912—the Granite Seminary in Salt Lake City.

I learned much from Brother Rich. He was a prominent and successful community and Church leader. He was never hesitant. He taught me to consider a problem, determine what gospel principle was involved, and then make a decision. His philosophy was simply "Do what is right; let the consequence follow" ("Do What Is Right," *Hymns* [1985], no. 237).

Brother Rich had lived through the history of seminary and talked freely about it. Through him I became acquainted with the "old warhorses," as he called them.

As I think back, a stream of memories comes forward. I recall William E. Berrett, who opened seminary in the Uintah Basin. During the summer, he walked from town to town recruiting students for his class. The Berretts' first child was born and buried there. Brother and Sister Berrett rode to the cemetery in the backseat of a car. On his lap was the little un-painted, wooden casket that he had built for their son.

Brother A. Theodore Tuttle and I also served together as supervisors over seminaries and institutes and later together as General Authorities.

Brother Tuttle had been a lieutenant in the marines. At the battle of Iwo Jima, he returned to the ship to get a large flag. On shore he handed it to a runner who took it to the top of Mount Suribachi and onto the pages of history. You may remember the famous picture of that flag being raised by ser-vicemen. That event was later cast in bronze as a memorial in Washington, D. C.

Another early teacher was Elijah Hicken, who was sent to the Big Horn Basin in Wyoming to open a seminary. He was unwelcome. They had run out the teacher before him—very rough class! They did not want him there and thought to run him out, as they had others before him. His life was actually threatened. The patriarch came to him with a blessing and a promise that his life would be protected. On the strength of that blessing, Brother Hicken took off the six-shooter he had worn to class each day, and seminary was planted there.

I also remember a tall, smiling J. Wiley Sessions, who opened the first institute of religion at Moscow, Idaho, in 1926.

Church Leaders Are Aware of You and Your Potential

Early in my years of teaching, I had a personal contact with Elder Harold B. Lee. I can remember standing with my wife outside the home of a counselor in our stake presidency, Eberhardt Zundel. I was serving as an assistant stake clerk. We were there for lunch between sessions of our stake conference. Elder Lee came out of the house and walked right up to me. I was speechless. There I was talking to an Apostle. (I have talked with a few other Apostles since that time!)

Elder Lee said, pointing to the Zundel home, "There are great men in there"—referring to the stake presidency. "You learn at their feet, and you will never be off course." I teared up just a little, and Elder Lee said: "God bless you, my boy. One day you will carry great responsibility in this Church." I suppose he said that to a lot of boys, but it had a profound effect on me. I remember the feeling I had in his presence.

A few years later I was speaking to seminary teachers in Salt Lake City. A call came telling me that I was to go immediately to the office of President David O. McKay. It was Saturday morning, and general conference was to convene shortly. I went quickly to President McKay's office.

There was an attendant there, and he said, "What are you doing here?"

I said, "President McKay sent for me."

He said, "That's what they all say! You sit right there."

I sat right there!

Soon President Hugh B. Brown, Counselor in the First Presidency, came through the corridor and said, "What are you doing here? Why are you sitting here?"

And I said, "I can't get in."

He said, "I'll fix that."

He ushered me into the office of President David O. McKay.

I went to sit across from his desk, and he motioned for me to come around. He had a chair behind his desk, facing him. President McKay took hold of both my hands and called me to be an Assistant to the Quorum of the Twelve Apostles. That was the closest I had ever been to the President of the Church.

A few minutes later he looked at his watch and said, "We must go now to the Tabernacle. Sister Packer will just have to learn about this as it comes out over the air." And she did!

Fifty years and more than 2.5 million miles of worldwide travel later, I have an ever-deepening interest in the seminary and institute programs and more particularly in the youth.

The Gift of the Holy Ghost Will Protect You in Enemy Territory

You have been taught all of your lives about the gift of the Holy Ghost, but teaching can only go so far. You can and, in fact, you must go the rest of the way alone to discover within yourself how the Holy Ghost can be a guiding and protective influence.

For young men and young women, the process is the same. Discovering how the Holy Ghost operates in your life is the quest of a lifetime. Once you have made that discovery for yourself, you can live in enemy territory and not be deceived or destroyed. No member of this Church—and that means each of you—will ever make a serious mistake without first being warned by the promptings of the Holy Ghost.

Sometimes when you have made a mistake, you may have

said afterward, "I knew I should not have done that. It did not feel right," or perhaps, "I knew I *should* have done that. I just did not have the courage to act!" Those impressions are the Holy Ghost attempting to direct you toward good or warning you away from harm.

The Holy Ghost will withdraw if you participate in immoral practices or fill your mind with such things that come when one watches pornography.

You can quickly learn to follow the promptings of the Holy Ghost. This power of revelation from the gift of the Holy Ghost operates on principles of righteousness.

There are certain things that you must not do if the lines of communication are to remain open. You cannot lie or cheat or steal or act immorally and have those channels remain free from disruption. Do not go where the environment resists spiritual communication. You must learn to seek the power and direction that is available to you, and then follow that course no matter what.

Prayer Is an Important Line of Communication

First on your "to do" list, put the word *prayer*. Most of the time your prayers will be silent. You can think a prayer.

Parents and teachers are concerned about the day that their children or youth are left on their own. You are never left outside the influence of a Heavenly Parent. He is our Father, and He is always there.

Sometimes it is hard for young people to confide in their parents. You can always have a direct line of communication

DISCOVERING

how

THE HOLY GHOST

OPERATES

IN YOUR LIFE

is

THE QUEST OF

A LIFETIME.

with your Father in Heaven. Do not allow the adversary to convince you that no one is listening on the other end. Your prayers are always heard. You are never alone!

Keep Your Spiritual Receptors Strong

Take care of your body. Be clean. "Know ye not that ye are the temple of God, and that the Spirit of God dwelleth in you?" (1 Corinthians 3:16).

The Prophet Joseph Smith received the Word of Wisdom by revelation. In simple terms: no tea, coffee, alcohol, or tobacco (see D&C 89:5–9). It was not known at that time that these things were bad for your health and can be addicting. The terrible plague of drug addiction was not understood then.

Read carefully the promises found in section 89 of the Doctrine and Covenants:

"All saints who remember to keep and do these sayings, walking in obedience to the commandments, shall receive health in their navel and marrow to their bones;

"And shall find wisdom and great treasures of knowledge, even hidden treasures;

"And shall run and not be weary, and shall walk and not faint" (D&C 89:18–20).

The Word of Wisdom does not promise perfect health but that the spiritual receptors within you might be strengthened. The certainty is that your body will, in due time, grow old and eventually become uninhabitable, and the spirit will be forced to leave. We call that death.

Stay away from tattoos and similar things that deface your

body. Do not do that which would dishonor yourself, your parents, or your Father in Heaven. Your body was created in His image.

Unworthy people can be uncomfortable in the presence of someone who is virtuous. Do not be embarrassed by the teasing you may get from those around you. In the end, many will understand and respect you for your values.

Prophetic Counsel Teaches What Is True

One thing that I have learned about young people through all of these years: You not only can take the truth, but you want to know the truth.

We know that gender was set in the premortal world (see "The Family: A Proclamation to the World," *Ensign*, November 2010, 129). "The spirit and the body are the soul of man" (D&C 88:15). This matter of gender is of great concern to the Brethren, as are all matters of morality.

A few of you may have felt or been told that you were born with troubling feelings and that you are not guilty if you act on those temptations. Doctrinally we know that if that were true your agency would have been erased, and that cannot happen. You always have a choice to follow the promptings of the Holy Ghost and live a morally pure and chaste life, one filled with virtue.

President Gordon B. Hinckley announced the following in a general conference:

"People inquire about our position on those who consider themselves . . . gays and lesbians. My response is that we love them as sons and daughters of God. They may have certain inclinations which are powerful and which may be difficult to control. Most people have inclinations of one kind or another at various times. If they do not act upon these inclinations, then they can go forward as do all other members of the Church. If they violate the law of chastity and the moral standards of the Church, then they are subject to the discipline of the Church, just as others are.

"We want to help . . . strengthen them, to assist them with their problems and to help them with their difficulties. But we cannot stand idle if they indulge in immoral activity, if they try to uphold and defend and live in a so-called same-sex marriage situation. To permit such would be to make light of the very serious and sacred foundation of God-sanctioned marriage and its very purpose, the rearing of families" ("What Are People Asking about Us?" *Ensign*, November 1998, 71).

President Hinckley was speaking for the Church.

Use Your Agency to Keep or Regain Safe Ground

The first gift that Adam and Eve received was agency: "Thou mayest choose for thyself, for it is given unto thee" (Moses 3:17).

You have that same agency. Use it wisely to deny acting on any impure impulse or unholy temptation that may come into your mind. Just do not go there, and if you are already there, come back out of it. "Deny yourselves of all ungodliness" (Moroni 10:32).

Do not tamper with the life-giving powers in your body

alone or with members of either gender. That is the standard of the Church, and it will not change. As you mature, there is a temptation to experiment or explore immoral activities. Do not do that!

It is natural to resist restraints of any kind. I realize that you do not like to be told what to do. But if immoral conduct is a temptation for you, I plead with you to do all in your power to overcome it, however difficult it may be.

The key word is *discipline*—self-discipline. The word *discipline* comes from the word *disciple* or *follower*. Be a disciple/follower of the Savior, and you will be safe.

One or two of you may be thinking, "I am already guilty of this or that serious mistake. It is too late for me." It is never too late.

You have been taught at home and in seminary about the Atonement of Jesus Christ. The Atonement is like an eraser. It can wipe away guilt and the effect of whatever it is that is causing you to feel guilty.

Guilt is spiritual pain. Do not suffer from chronic pain. Get rid of it. Be done with it. Repent, and, if necessary, repent again and again and again and again until you—not the enemy—are in charge of you.

Lasting Peace Comes by Repenting Often

Life turns out to be a succession of trials and errors. Add "repent often" to your list of things to do. This will bring you lasting peace that cannot be purchased at any earthly price.

Understanding the Atonement may be the one most important truth that you can learn in your youth.

If you are associating with others who drag you down instead of building you up, stop and change company. You may be alone and lonely at times. The important question may be asked then, "When you are alone, are you in good company?" If you are doing something that you know is wrong, stop it. Stop it now.

Unwinding a bad habit that you have allowed to entangle you can be very difficult. But the power is in you to do it. Do not despair.

It is not likely that you will ever have a personal encounter with the adversary; he does not show himself that way. But even if he came personally to you to test and tempt you, you have an advantage. You can assert your agency, and he will have to leave you alone.

It is not easy. Life is not guaranteed to be either easy or fair. That is the test.

When you choose to repent, you will receive a testimony and know that the gospel is true. You will know what the Lord meant when He promised, "Though your sins be as scarlet, they shall be as white as snow; though they be red like crimson, they shall be as wool" (Isaiah 1:18). And then this great scripture: "And [He] will remember [your sins] no more" (Jeremiah 31:34). So why don't you "not remember" them.

Take Advantage of the Blessings of Seminary

You are not ordinary. You are very special. You are exceptional. How do I know that? I know that because you were born at a time and in a place where the gospel of Jesus Christ can come into your life through the teachings and activities of your home and of The Church of Jesus Christ of Latter-day Saints. It is, as the Lord Himself has said, "the only true and living church upon the face of the whole earth" (D&C 1:30).

There are other things we could add to the list, but you know what you should and should not be doing in your life. You know right and wrong and do not need to be commanded in all things.

Do not squander your years of seminary instruction. Take advantage of the great blessing you have to learn the doctrines of the Church and the teachings of the prophets. Learn that which is of most worth. It will bless you and your posterity for many generations to come.

Alma commanded his son Helaman: "O, remember, my son, and learn wisdom in thy youth; yea, learn in thy youth to keep the commandments of God" (Alma 37:35).

People now, to a large extent, are tempted to surrender their agency or independence and replace it with the word *entitlement*. They expect that everything will be freely provided for them. If that pattern is in your thinking, get rid of it. If you want to be happy, you must pay the price through obedience. The restraints that you face against wrongdoing are an enormous protection for you.

When our children were little, they would sometimes say, "Do I *have* to do that?" The answer is, "No, you do not have to. You *get* to."

Once you have this self-control in your life, you will not need to be told what to do all of the time. You will find your way and know where you fit in.

Some of you are floundering about and struggling to find what you will do. It does not really matter what you choose to do for a living. What matters is what you will *be*. You have the guidelines to know that. Remember the Spirit is always with you to teach you.

Not many years will pass until you are married and have children, a marriage that should be sealed in the temple. Our prayer is that you will find yourself, in due time, safely settled in a family ward or branch. You will find that you will learn more from your children than ever they will learn from you.

Go Forward with Hope and Faith

Do not fear the future. Do not fear what is ahead. Go forward with hope and faith. Remember that supernal gift of the Holy Ghost. Learn to be taught by it. Learn to seek it. Learn to live by it. Learn to pray always in the name of Jesus Christ (see 3 Nephi 18:19–20). The Spirit of the Lord will attend you, and you will be blessed.

The poet wrote:

> *So nigh is grandeur to our dust,*
> *So near is God to man,*

When Duty whispers low, Thou must,
The youth replies, I can.
(Ralph Waldo Emerson, "Voluntaries,"
   in *The Complete Writings of Ralph Waldo*
   Emerson [1929], 895)

We have a deep and profound faith in you.

I bear my testimony to you—a witness that came to me in my youth. And you are no different from anyone else than I am. You have as much right to that testimony and witness as anyone. It will come to you if you earn it. I invoke the blessings of the Lord upon you—the blessings of that witness to be in your life, to guide you as you make a happy future.

Part Four

The Scriptures—
The Key to
Spiritual
Protection

CHAPTER 15

The Key to Spiritual Protection

A short time ago, I sealed a young couple in the temple. This couple had kept themselves worthy to arrive at the marvelous day when a son and a daughter leave the homes of their youth and become husband and wife. On this sacred occasion, they were pure and clean. In due course, they will begin to raise children of their own, consistent with the pattern established by our Father in Heaven. Their happiness, and the happiness of future generations, depends upon their living those standards established by the Savior and set forth in His scriptures.

Parents today wonder if there is a safe place to raise children. There *is* a safe place. It is in a gospel-centered home. We focus on the family in the Church, and we counsel parents everywhere to raise their children in righteousness.

From a talk given at general conference, October 2013.

The Apostle Paul prophesied and warned that "in the last days perilous times shall come.

"For men shall be lovers of their own selves, covetous, boasters, proud, blasphemers, disobedient to parents, unthankful, unholy,

"Without natural affection, trucebreakers, false accusers, incontinent, fierce, despisers of those that are good,

"Traitors, heady, highminded, lovers of pleasures more than lovers of God;

"Having a form of godliness, but denying the power thereof: from such turn away" (2 Timothy 3:1–5).

Paul also prophesied, "Evil men and seducers shall wax worse and worse, deceiving, and being deceived" (2 Timothy 3:13).

These verses serve as a warning, showing which patterns to avoid. We must be ever watchful and diligent. We can review each of these prophecies and put a check mark by them as being present and of concern in the world today:

Perilous times—present. We live in very precarious times.

Covetous, boasters, proud—all are present and among us.

Blasphemers, disobedient to parents, unthankful, unholy, without natural affection—all of these are well accounted for.

Trucebreakers, false accusers, and so on—all can be checked off against the prevailing evidence that exists all around us.

Moroni also spoke of the wickedness of our day when he warned:

"When ye shall see these things come among you . . . ye shall awake to a sense of your awful situation. . . .

"Wherefore, I, Moroni, am commanded to write these things that evil may be done away, and that the time may come that Satan may have no power upon the hearts of the children of men, but that they may be persuaded to do good continually, that they may come unto the fountain of all righteousness and be saved" (Ether 8:24, 26).

The descriptions Paul and Moroni give of our day are so accurate that they cannot be dismissed. For many it may be quite disturbing, even discouraging. Nevertheless, when I think of the future, I am overwhelmed with feelings of positive optimism.

In Paul's revelation, in addition to the list of challenges and problems, he also tells us what we can do to protect ourselves:

"Continue thou in the things which thou hast learned and hast been assured of, knowing of whom thou hast learned them;

"And that from a child thou hast known the holy scriptures, which are able to make thee wise unto salvation through faith which is in Christ Jesus" (2 Timothy 3:14–15).

The scriptures hold the keys to spiritual protection. They contain the doctrine and laws and ordinances that will bring each child of God to a testimony of Jesus Christ as the Savior and Redeemer.

With years of preparation, there has been an enormous effort to produce the scriptures in every language, with footnotes and cross-references. We seek to make them available to all who wish to learn. They teach us where to go and what to do. They offer hope and knowledge.

Years ago, Elder S. Dilworth Young of the Seventy taught

me a lesson about reading the scriptures. A stake was struggling with tensions and difficulties among the members, and counsel needed to be given.

I asked President Young, "What should I say?"

He answered simply, "Tell them to read the scriptures."

I asked, "Which scriptures?"

He said, "It really doesn't matter. Tell them to open up the Book of Mormon, for instance, and begin to read. Soon the feeling of peace and inspiration will come, and a solution will present itself."

Make scripture reading a part of your regular routine, and the blessings will follow. There is in the scriptures a voice of warning, but there is also great nourishment.

If the language of the scriptures at first seems strange to you, keep reading. Soon you will come to recognize the beauty and power found on those pages.

Paul said, "All scripture is given by inspiration of God, and is profitable for doctrine, for reproof, for correction, for instruction in righteousness" (2 Timothy 3:16).

You can test this promise for yourself.

We live in perilous times; nevertheless, we can find hope and peace for ourselves and for our families. Those living in sorrow, despairing at the possibility of children being rescued from where the world has taken them, must never give up. "Be not afraid, only believe" (Mark 5:36). Righteousness is more powerful than wickedness.

Children taught an understanding of the scriptures early in life will come to know the path they should walk and will be more inclined to remain on that path. Those who stray will

Peace

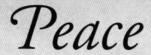

can be settled in the heart

of each who turns to the

scriptures and unlocks

THE PROMISES OF

PROTECTION

AND REDEMPTION

that are taught therein.

have the ability to return and, with help, can find their way back.

The sons of Mosiah fought against the Church for a time but later repented and underwent a dramatic change. In Alma we read, "These sons of Mosiah . . . had waxed strong in the knowledge of the truth; for they were men of a sound understanding and they had searched the scriptures diligently, that they might know the word of God" (Alma 17:2).

President Joseph F. Smith was five years old when his father, Hyrum, was killed in Carthage Jail. Later, Joseph crossed the plains with his widowed mother.

At age fifteen he was called on a mission to Hawaii. He felt lost and alone and said: "I was very much oppressed. . . . I felt as if I was so debased in my condition of poverty, lack of intelligence and knowledge, just a boy, that I hardly dared look [anyone] in the face."

While pondering his plight one night, young Joseph dreamed he was on a journey, rushing as fast as he possibly could. He carried with him a small bundle. Finally, he came to a wonderful mansion, which was his destination. As he approached, he saw a sign which read, "Bath." He quickly went in and washed himself. He opened his little bundle and found clean, white clothing—"a thing," he said, "I had not seen for a long time." He put them on and rushed to the door of the mansion.

"I knocked," he said, "and the door opened, and the man who stood there was the Prophet Joseph Smith. He looked at me a little reprovingly, and the first words he said [were]: 'Joseph, you are late.' Yet I took confidence and said:

"'Yes, but I am clean—I am clean!'" (Joseph F. Smith, *Gospel Doctrine,* 5th ed. [1939], 542).

And so it can be for each of us.

If you are set on a course of faith and activity in the Church, stay on course and keep your covenants. Continue forward until the time when the Lord's blessings will come to you and the Holy Ghost will be revealed as a moving force in your life.

If you are presently on a course that points away from the one outlined in the scriptures, let me assure you there is a way back.

Jesus Christ has prescribed a very clear method for us to repent and find healing in our lives. The cure for most mistakes can be found by seeking forgiveness through personal prayer. However, there are certain spiritual illnesses, particularly those dealing with violations of the moral law, which absolutely require the assistance and treatment of a qualified spiritual physician.

Years ago there came to my office a young woman and her aging father. She had brought him several hundred miles to find a remedy for the guilt he felt. As a young man he had made a serious mistake, and in his old age the memory came back to him. He could not shake the feeling of guilt. He could not go back and undo the problem of his youth on his own, but he could start where he was and, with help, erase the guilt which had followed him all those years.

I was grateful that by teaching him principles from the Book of Mormon, it was as though a tremendous weight was lifted from his shoulders. When he and his daughter drove back home those many miles, the old man had left behind the guilt of the past transgression.

If you "awake to a sense of your awful situation" (Ether 8:24) and wish to return to full spiritual health, see your bishop. He holds the keys and can help you along the pathway of repentance.

Just as chalk can be removed from a blackboard, with sincere repentance the effects of our transgression can be erased through the Atonement of Jesus Christ. That promise applies in every case.

The gospel teaches us to be happy, to have faith rather than fear, to find hope and overcome despair, to leave darkness and turn toward the light of the everlasting gospel.

Paul and others warned about the trials of our time and the days yet to come. But peace can be settled in the heart of each who turns to the scriptures and unlocks the promises of protection and redemption that are taught therein. We invite all to turn to the Savior Jesus Christ, to His teachings as found in the Old Testament, the New Testament, the Book of Mormon, the Doctrine and Covenants, and the Pearl of Great Price.

I bear certain witness of the scriptures as a key to our spiritual protection. I also bear witness of the healing power of the Atonement of Jesus Christ, "that through him all might be saved" (D&C 76:42) who will be saved. The Lord's Church has been established on the earth once again. Of the truthfulness of the gospel I bear witness. Of Him I am a witness.

CHAPTER 16

———◦◦◦———

Guided by
the Holy Spirit

It has been four hundred years since the publication of
the King James Bible, with significant contributions from
William Tyndale, a great hero in my eyes.

The clergy did not want the Bible published in common
English. They hounded Tyndale from place to place. He said
to them, "If God spare my life, ere many years I will cause a
boy that driveth the plough shall know more of the Scripture
than thou" (in David Daniell, introduction to *Tyndale's New
Testament* [1989], viii).

Tyndale was betrayed and confined to a dark, freezing
prison in Brussels for over a year. His clothing was in rags. He
begged his captors for his coat and cap and a candle, saying, "It
is indeed wearisome sitting alone in the dark" (in Daniell, introduction to *Tyndale's New Testament*, ix). These were denied

---

From a talk given at general conference, April 2011.

him. Eventually, he was taken from prison and before a large crowd was strangled and burned at the stake. But William Tyndale's work and martyr's death were not in vain.

Since Latter-day Saint children are taught from their youth to know the scriptures, they in a measure fulfill the prophecy made four centuries earlier by William Tyndale.

Our scriptures today consist of the Bible, the Book of Mormon: Another Testament of Jesus Christ, the Pearl of Great Price, and the Doctrine and Covenants.

Because of the Book of Mormon, we are frequently called the Mormon Church, a title we do not resent, but it is really not accurate.

In the Book of Mormon, the Lord revisited the Nephites because they prayed to the Father in His name. And the Lord said:

"What will ye that I shall give unto you?

"And they said unto him: Lord, we will that thou wouldst tell us the name whereby we shall call this church; for there are disputations among the people concerning this matter.

"And the Lord said . . . , why is it that the people should murmur and dispute because of this thing?

"Have they not read the scriptures, which say ye must take upon you the name of Christ . . . ? For by this name shall ye be called at the last day. . . .

"Therefore, whatsoever ye shall do, ye shall do it in my name; therefore ye shall call the church in my name; and ye shall call upon the Father in my name that he will bless the church for my sake.

"And how be it my church save it be called in my name?

For if a church be called in Moses' name then it be Moses' church; or if it be called in the name of a man then it be the church of a man; but if it be called in my name then it is my church, if it so be that they are built upon my gospel" (3 Nephi 27:2–5, 7–8).

Obedient to revelation, we call ourselves The Church of Jesus Christ of Latter-day Saints rather than the Mormon Church. It is one thing for others to refer to the Church as the Mormon Church or to us as Mormons; it is quite another for us to do so.

The First Presidency stated:

"The use of the revealed name, The Church of Jesus Christ of Latter-day Saints (D&C 115:4), is increasingly important in our responsibility to proclaim the name of the Savior throughout all the world. Accordingly, we ask that when we refer to the Church we use its full name wherever possible. . . .

"When referring to Church members, we suggest 'members of The Church of Jesus Christ of Latter-day Saints.' As a shortened reference, 'Latter-day Saints' is preferred" (First Presidency letter, February 23, 2001).

As Latter-day Saints, "We talk of Christ, we rejoice in Christ, we preach of Christ, we prophesy of Christ, and we write according to our prophecies, that our children may know to what source they may look for a remission of their sins" (2 Nephi 25:26).

The world will refer to us as they will, but in our speech, always remember that we belong to the Church of *Jesus Christ*.

Some claim we are not Christians. They either do not know us at all or they misunderstand.

In the Church every ordinance is done by the authority of and in the name of Jesus Christ. We have the same organization as did the primitive Church, with apostles and prophets (see Articles of Faith 1:6).

Anciently the Lord called and ordained Twelve Apostles. He was betrayed and crucified. After His Resurrection, the Savior taught His disciples for forty days and then ascended into heaven (see Acts 1:3–11).

But something was missing. A few days later the Twelve gathered in a house, and "suddenly there came a sound from heaven as of a rushing mighty wind, and it filled all the house. . . . Cloven tongues . . . of fire [rested] upon each of them. And they were . . . filled with the Holy Ghost" (Acts 2:2–4). His Apostles were now empowered. They understood that the authority given by the Savior and the gift of the Holy Ghost were essential for the establishment of His Church. They were commanded to baptize and confer the gift of the Holy Ghost (see Acts 2:38).

In time the Apostles and the priesthood they carried were gone. The authority and power to administer had to be restored. For centuries men looked forward to the return of the authority and the establishment of the Lord's Church.

In 1829 the priesthood was restored to Joseph Smith and Oliver Cowdery by John the Baptist and the Apostles Peter, James, and John. Now worthy male members of the Church are ordained to the priesthood. This authority and the attendant gift of the Holy Ghost, which is conferred upon all members of the Church after baptism, set us apart from other churches.

If someone is looking for a
church that requires very little,
this is not the one.

IT IS NOT EASY TO BE A

Latter-day Saint,

but in the long run it is

the only true course.

An early revelation directs "that every man might speak in the name of God the Lord, even the Savior of the world" (D&C 1:20). The work in the Church today is performed by ordinary men and women called and sustained to preside, to teach, and to administer. It is by the power of revelation and the gift of the Holy Ghost that those called are guided to know the Lord's will. Others may not accept such things as prophecy, revelation, and the gift of the Holy Ghost, but if they are to understand us at all, they must understand that we accept those things.

The Lord revealed to Joseph Smith a code of health, the Word of Wisdom, long before the dangers were known to the world. All are taught to avoid tea, coffee, liquor, tobacco, and of course varieties of drugs and addictive substances, which are ever present before our young people. Those who obey this revelation are promised that they "shall receive health in their navel and marrow to their bones;

"And shall find wisdom and great treasures of knowledge, even hidden treasures;

"And shall run and not be weary, and shall walk and not faint" (D&C 89:18–20).

In another revelation, the Lord's standard of morality commands that the sacred powers to beget life be protected and employed only between man and woman, husband and wife (see "The Family: A Proclamation to the World," *Ensign*, November 2010, 129). To misuse this power is exceeded in seriousness only by the shedding of innocent blood and denying the Holy Ghost (see Alma 39:4–6). If one transgresses the law, the doctrine of repentance teaches how to erase the effect of this transgression.

Everyone is tested. One might think it is unfair to be singled out and subjected to a particular temptation, but this is the purpose of mortal life—to be tested. And the answer is the same for everyone: we must, and we can, resist temptations of any kind.

"The great plan of happiness" (Alma 42:8) centers on family life. The husband is the head of the home and the wife the heart of the home. And marriage is an equal partnership. A Latter-day Saint man is a responsible family man, faithful in the gospel. He is a caring, devoted husband and father. He reveres womanhood. The wife sustains her husband. Both parents nurture the spiritual growth of their children.

Latter-day Saints are taught to love one another and to frankly forgive offenses.

My life was changed by a saintly patriarch. He married his sweetheart. They were deeply in love, and soon she was expecting their first child.

The night the baby was born, there were complications. The only doctor was somewhere in the countryside tending to the sick. After many hours of labor, the condition of the mother-to-be became desperate. Finally, the doctor was located. In the emergency, he acted quickly and soon the baby was born, and the crisis, it appeared, was over. But some days later, the young mother died from the very infection that the doctor had been treating at another home that night.

The young man's world was shattered. As the weeks wore on, his grief festered. He thought of little else, and in his bitterness he became threatening. Today, no doubt, he would have been pressed to file a malpractice suit, as though money would solve anything.

One night a knock came at his door. A little girl said simply, "Daddy wants you to come over. He wants to talk to you."

"Daddy" was the stake president. The counsel from that wise leader was simply "John, leave it alone. Nothing you do about it will bring her back. Anything you do will make it worse. John, leave it alone."

This had been my friend's trial. How could he leave it alone? A terrible wrong had been committed. He struggled to get hold of himself and finally determined that he should be obedient and follow the counsel of that wise stake president. He would leave it alone.

He said, "I was an old man before I understood and could finally see a poor country doctor—overworked, underpaid, run ragged from patient to patient, with little medicine, no hospital, few instruments, struggling to save lives, and succeeding for the most part. He had come in a moment of crisis, when two lives hung in the balance, and had acted without delay. I finally understood!" He said, "I would have ruined my life and the lives of others."

Many times he had thanked the Lord on his knees for a wise priesthood leader who counseled simply, "John, leave it alone."

Around us we see members of the Church who have become offended. Some take offense at incidents in the history of the Church or its leaders and suffer their whole lives, unable to get past the mistakes of others. They do not leave it alone. They fall into inactivity.

That attitude is somewhat like a man being hit by a club. Offended, he takes up a club and beats himself over the head with it all the days of his life. How foolish! How sad! That kind of revenge is self-inflicting. If you have been offended, forgive, forget it, and leave it alone.

The Book of Mormon carries this warning: "And now, if there are faults they are the mistakes of men; wherefore, condemn not the things of God, that ye may be found spotless at the judgment-seat of Christ" (Title page of the Book of Mormon).

A Latter-day Saint is quite an ordinary individual. We are now everywhere in the world, millions of us, and this is only the beginning. We are taught to be in the world but not of the world (see John 17:14–19). Therefore, we live ordinary lives in ordinary families mixed in with the general population.

We are taught not to lie or steal or cheat (see Exodus 20:15–16). We do not use profanity. We are positive and happy and not afraid of life.

We are "willing to mourn with those that mourn . . . and comfort those that stand in need of comfort, and to stand as witnesses of God at all times and in all things, and in all places" (Mosiah 18:9).

If someone is looking for a church that requires very little, this is not the one. It is not easy to be a Latter-day Saint, but in the long run it is the only true course.

Regardless of opposition or "wars, rumors of wars, and earthquakes in divers places" (Mormon 8:30), no power or influence can stop this work. Every one of us can be guided by the spirit of revelation and the gift of the Holy Ghost. "As well might man stretch forth his puny arm to stop the Missouri river in its decreed course, or to turn it up stream, as to hinder the Almighty from pouring down knowledge from heaven upon the heads of the Latter-day Saints" (D&C 121:33).

If you are carrying some burden, forget it, let it alone. Do a lot of forgiving and a little repenting, and you will be visited by the Spirit of the Holy Ghost and confirmed by the testimony that you did not know existed. You will be watched over and blessed—you and yours. This is an invitation to come unto Him.

CHAPTER 17

Another Testament of Jesus Christ

I have been privileged to hold in my hands a first-edition copy of the Book of Mormon. It was printed in 1830 on a hand-operated letter press at the E. B. Grandin Company in the village of Palmyra, New York.

In June of 1829, Joseph Smith, then twenty-three years old, called on twenty-three-year-old Mr. Grandin in company with Martin Harris, a local farmer. Mr. Grandin had three months earlier advertised his intent to publish books. Joseph Smith provided pages of a handwritten manuscript.

If the content of the book did not doom it to remain obscure, the account of where it came from certainly would. Imagine an angel directing a teenage boy to the woods where he found buried a stone vault and a set of golden plates.

The writings on the plates were translated by use of a Urim

From a talk given at general conference, October 2001.

and Thummim, which is referred to a number of times in the Old Testament (see Ex. 28:30; Lev. 8:8; Num. 27:21; Deut. 33:8; 1 Sam. 28:6; Ezra 2:63; Neh. 7:65) and described by Hebrew scholars as an instrument "whereby the revelation was given and truth declared" (John M'Clintock and James Strong, *Cyclopedia of Biblical, Theological, and Ecclesiastical Literature* [1867–1881], s.v. "Urim and Thummim").

Before the book was off the press, pages of it were stolen and printed in the local newspaper, accompanied by ridicule. Opposition was destined to excite mobs to kill the Prophet Joseph Smith and drive those who believed him into the wilderness.

From that very unlikely beginning to this day, well over 100 million copies of the Book of Mormon: Another Testament of Jesus Christ have been printed. It has been published in sixty-two languages, with selections of it in another thirty-seven languages, and twenty-two translations are in process.

Now tens of thousands of full-time missionaries in 162 countries pay their own way to devote up to two years of their lives to testify that the Book of Mormon is true.

For generations it has inspired those who read it. Herbert Schreiter had read his German translation of the Book of Mormon. In it he read:

"When ye shall receive these things, I would exhort you that ye would ask God, the Eternal Father, in the name of Christ, if these things are not true; and if ye shall ask with a sincere heart, with real intent, having faith in Christ, he will manifest the truth of it unto you, by the power of the Holy Ghost.

"And by the power of the Holy Ghost ye may know the truth of all things" (Moro. 10:4–5).

Herbert Schreiter tested the promise and joined The Church of Jesus Christ of Latter-day Saints.

In 1946, released as a prisoner of war, Herbert returned to his wife and three little daughters in Leipzig, Germany. Soon thereafter, he went as a missionary to Bernburg, Germany. Alone, without a companion, he sat cold and hungry in a room, wondering how he should begin.

He thought of what he had to offer the war-devastated people. He printed by hand a placard that read, "Will there be a further life after death?" and posted it on a wall.

About that same time, a family from a small village in Poland came to Bernburg.

Manfred Schütze was four years old. His father had been killed in the war. His mother, with his grandparents, and his mother's sister, also a widow, and her two little girls, were forced to evacuate their village with only thirty minutes' notice. They grabbed what they could and headed west. Manfred and his mother pulled and pushed a small cart. At times, the ailing grandfather rode in the cart. One Polish officer looked at the pathetic little Manfred and began to weep.

At the border, soldiers ransacked their belongings and threw their bedding into the river. Manfred and his mother were then separated from the family. His mother wondered if they might have gone to Bernburg, where her grandmother was born, perhaps to relatives there. After weeks of unbelievable suffering, they arrived in Bernburg and found the family.

The seven of them lived together in one small room. But

their troubles were not over. The mother of the two little girls died. The grieving grandmother cried out for a preacher, and asked, "Will I see my family again?"

The preacher answered, "My dear lady, there is no such thing as the Resurrection. They who are dead are dead!"

They wrapped the body in a paper bag for burial.

On the way from the grave, the grandfather talked of taking their own lives, as many others had done. Just then they saw the placard that Elder Schreiter had posted on the building—"Is there further life after death?"—with an invitation from The Church of Jesus Christ of Latter-day Saints. At a meeting, they learned of the Book of Mormon: Another Testament of Jesus Christ.

The book explains:

- The purpose of mortal life and death (see 2 Ne. 2:21; 33:9; Alma 12:24; 34:32; 42:4),
- The certainty of life after death (see 2 Ne. 9:3–7; Mosiah 16:8; 3 Ne. 11),
- What happens when the spirit leaves the body (see Alma 34:34; 40:11–14, 21),
- The description of the Resurrection (see 2 Ne. 9:12; Alma 40:23; 41:2; 3 Ne. 11:1–16),
- How to receive and retain a remission of your sins (see Mosiah 4:1–3, 12, 26; Alma 4:14),
- What hold justice or mercy may have on you (see Alma 34:15–16; 41:14; 42:15–16, 22–25),
- What to pray for (see 2 Ne. 4:35; 32:8–9; Enos 1:9;

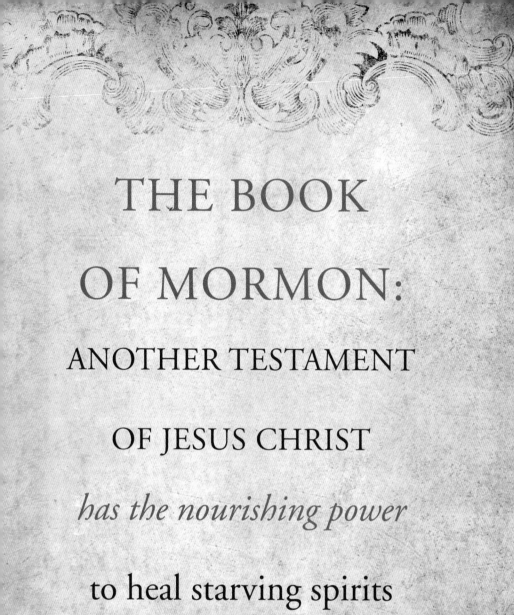

THE BOOK
OF MORMON:

ANOTHER TESTAMENT

OF JESUS CHRIST

has the nourishing power

to heal starving spirits

of the world.

Alma 13:28; 34:17–27, 37:36–37; 3 Ne. 18:19–21; Moro. 7:26),

- Priesthood (see 2 Ne. 6:2; Mosiah 18:18; Alma 6:1; 13; 3 Ne. 11:21; 18:37; Moro. 2:2; 3:4),

- Covenants and ordinances (see 2 Ne. 11:5; Mosiah 5:5; 18:13; Alma 13:8, 16),

- The office and ministry of angels (see 2 Ne. 32:2–3; Omni 1:25; Moro. 7:25, 37),

- The still, small voice of personal revelation (see 1 Ne. 16:9; 17:44–45; Enos 1:10; Alma 32:23; Hel. 5:30; 3 Ne. 11:3),

- Preeminently, the mission of Jesus Christ (see 1 Ne. 11:13–33; 2 Ne. 2:6–10; Mosiah 3:5–12; Alma 7:7–13; 3 Ne. 27:13–16),

- And many other jewels that make up the fulness of the gospel of Jesus Christ.

They joined the Church. Soon their lives changed. The grandfather found work as a baker and could provide bread for his family and also for Elder Schreiter, who had given them "the bread of life" (John 6:35).

Then help came from the Church in the United States. Manfred grew up eating grain out of little sacks with a picture of a beehive on them and peaches from California. He wore clothes from the welfare supplies of the Church.

Soon after I was released from the air force, I went to the welfare mill at Kaysville, Utah, to help fill bags of wheat for shipment to the starving people in Europe. I like to think one of the bags of grain that I filled myself went to Manfred Schütze and his mother. If not, it went to others in equal need.

President Dieter F. Uchtdorf remembers to this very day the smell of the grain and the feel of it in his little-boy hands. Perhaps one of the bags I filled reached his family.

When I was about ten, I made my first attempt to read the Book of Mormon. The first part was easy-flowing New Testament language. Then I came to the writings of the Old Testament prophet Isaiah. I could not understand them; I found them difficult to read. I laid the book aside.

I made other attempts to read the Book of Mormon. I did not read it all until I was on a troop ship with other bomber crew members, headed for the war in the Pacific. I determined that I would read the Book of Mormon and find out for myself whether it is true or not. Carefully I read and reread the book. I tested the promise that it contained. That was a life-changing event. After that, I never set the book aside.

Many young people have done better than I did.

A fifteen-year-old son of a mission president attended high school with very few members of the Church. One day the class was given a true or false test. Matthew was confident that he knew the answers to all except for question 15. It read, "Joseph Smith, the alleged Mormon prophet, wrote the Book of Mormon. True or false?"

He could not answer it either way, so being a clever teenager, he rewrote the question. He crossed out the word *alleged* and replaced the word *wrote* with *translated*. It then read, "Joseph Smith, the Mormon prophet, translated the Book of Mormon." He marked it true and handed it in.

The next day the teacher sternly asked why he had changed the question. He smiled and said, "Because Joseph Smith did not *write* the Book of Mormon, he *translated* it, and he was not an *alleged* prophet, he *was* a prophet."

He was then invited to tell the class how he knew that (see George D. Durrant, "Helping Your Children Be Missionaries," *Ensign,* Oct. 1977, 67).

In England, my wife and I became acquainted with Dorothy James, the widow of a clergyman who lived at the Close of Winchester Cathedral. She brought out a family Bible that had been lost for many years.

Years before, the possessions of a family member had been sold. The new owner found the Bible in a small desk that had remained unopened for over twenty years. There were also some letters written by a child named Beaumont James. He was able to find the James family and return the long-lost family Bible.

On the title page my wife read the following handwritten note: "This Bible has been in our family since the time of Thomas James in 1683 who was a lineal descendant of Thomas James first librarian of the Bodleian Library at Oxford, who was buried in New College Chapel August 1629. [Signed] C. T. C. James, 1880."

The margins and the open pages were completely filled with notations written in English, Latin, Greek, and Hebrew. One entry particularly touched her. From the bottom of the title page, she read, "The fairest Impression of the Bible is to have it well printed on the Readers heart."

And then this quote from Corinthians: "Ye are our epistle

written in our hearts, known and read of all men: Forasmuch as ye are manifestly declared to be the epistle of Christ ministered by us, written not with ink, but with the Spirit of the living God; not in tables of stone, but in fleshy tables of the heart. 2 Cor. 3:2–3" (as quoted in Donna Smith Packer, *On Footings from the Past: The Packers in England* [1988], 329).

My Book of Mormon also has many notes in the margins and is heavily underlined. I was in Florida once with President Gordon B. Hinckley. He turned from the pulpit and asked for a copy of the scriptures. I handed him my copy. He thumbed through it for a few seconds, turned, and handed it back, saying, "I can't read this. You have got everything crossed out!"

Amos prophesied of "a famine in the land, not a famine of bread, nor a thirst for water, but of hearing the words of the Lord" (Amos 8:11).

In a world ever more dangerous than the world of little Manfred Schütze and Dieter Uchtdorf, the Book of Mormon: Another Testament of Jesus Christ has the nourishing power to heal starving spirits of the world.

With Elder Walter F. González, a new member of the Seventy from Uruguay, I attended a conference in Moroni, Utah, a town with a Book of Mormon name. There is no doctor or dentist in Moroni. They must leave town to shop for groceries. Their students are bussed to a consolidated high school across the valley.

We held a meeting with 236 present. Lest Elder González see only ordinary rural farmers, I gave this sentence of testimony: "I know the gospel is true and that Jesus is the Christ." I asked if someone could repeat it in Spanish. Several hands went up. Could someone repeat it in another language? It was repeated in:

- Japanese
- Spanish
- German
- Portuguese
- Russian
- Chinese
- Tongan
- Italian
- Tagalog
- Dutch
- Finnish
- Maori
- Polish
- Korean
- French

That was fifteen languages!

Again in English: I know the gospel is true and that Jesus is the Christ.

I love this Book of Mormon: Another Testament of Jesus Christ. Study it and one can understand both the Old Testament and the New Testament in the Bible. I know it is true.

CHAPTER 18

Plain and Precious Things

Joseph Smith said, "I told the brethren that the Book of Mormon was the most correct of any book on earth, and the keystone of our religion, and a man would get nearer to God by abiding by its precepts, than by any other book" (Book of Mormon introduction).

The first edition of the Book of Mormon: Another Testament of Jesus Christ came off the press in Palmyra, New York, in March of 1830. Joseph Smith—an uneducated country boy—had just passed his twenty-fourth birthday. The year before, he had spent a total of about sixty-five days translating the plates. Almost half of it was after he had received the priesthood. The printing had taken seven months.

When I first read the Book of Mormon from cover to cover, I read the promise that if I "would ask God, the Eternal

From a talk given at general conference, April 2005.

Father, in the name of Christ, if [the things I had read were] true; and if [I would] ask with a sincere heart, with real intent, having faith in Christ, he [would] manifest the truth of it unto [me], by the power of the Holy Ghost" (Moroni 10:4). I tried to follow those instructions, as I understood them.

If I expected a glorious manifestation to come at once as an overpowering experience, it did not happen. Nevertheless, it felt good, and I began to believe.

The next verse has an even greater promise: "By the power of the Holy Ghost ye may know the truth of *all* things" (Moroni 10:5; emphasis added). I did not know how the Holy Ghost worked, even though the Book of Mormon explains it a number of times in a number of ways.

I also read, "If ye will enter in by the way, and receive the Holy Ghost, it will show unto you all things what ye should do" (2 Nephi 32:5). I had already done that when I was confirmed a member of the Church by the "Laying on of hands for the gift of the Holy Ghost" (Articles of Faith 1:4).

If I had expected in my little-boy innocence some special spiritual experience, it had not happened. Over the years as I listened to sermons and lessons and read in the Book of Mormon, I began to understand.

Nephi had been very badly treated by his brothers and reminded them that an angel had spoken unto them, "but ye were past feeling, that ye could not feel his words" (1 Nephi 17:45). When I understood that the Holy Ghost could communicate through our feelings, I understood why the words of Christ, whether from the New Testament or the Book of Mormon or the other scriptures, carried such a good feeling.

In time, I found that the scriptures had answers to things I needed to know.

I read, "Now these are the words, and ye may liken them unto you and unto all men" (2 Nephi 11:8; see also 1 Nephi 19:23–24; 2 Nephi 6:5; 11:2). I took that to mean that the scriptures are likened to me personally, and that is true of everyone else.

When a verse I had passed over several times took on personal meaning, I thought whoever wrote that verse had a deep and mature understanding of my life and how I felt.

For example, I read that the prophet Lehi partook of the fruit of the tree of life and said, "Wherefore, I began to be desirous that my family should partake of it also; for I knew that it was desirable above all other fruit" (1 Nephi 8:12). I had read that more than once. It did not mean much to me.

The prophet Nephi also said that he had written "the things of my soul . . . for the learning and the profit of my children" (2 Nephi 4:15). I had read that before, and it did not mean all that much to me, either. But later, when we had children, I understood that both Lehi and Nephi felt just as deeply about their children as we feel about our children and grandchildren.

I found these scriptures to be plain and precious. I wondered how young Joseph Smith could have such insights. The fact is I do not believe he had such penetrating insights. He did not have to have them. He just translated what was written on the plates.

Such plain and precious insights are everywhere in the Book

of Mormon. They reflect a depth of wisdom and experience that is certainly not characteristic of a twenty-three-year-old.

I learned that anyone, anywhere, could read in the Book of Mormon and receive inspiration.

Some insights came after reading a second, even a third time and seemed to be "likened" to what I faced in everyday life.

I mention another plain and precious insight that did not come with the first reading in the Book of Mormon. When I was eighteen years old, I was inducted into the military. While I had no reason to wonder about it before, I became very concerned if it was right for me to go to war. In time, I found my answer in the Book of Mormon:

"They [the Nephites] were not fighting for monarchy nor power but they were fighting for their homes and their liberties, their wives and their children, and their all, yea, for their rites of worship and their church.

"And they were doing that which they felt was the duty which they owed to their God; for the Lord had said unto them, and also unto their fathers, that: Inasmuch as ye are not guilty of the first offense, neither the second, ye shall not suffer yourselves to be slain by the hands of your enemies.

"And again, the Lord has said that: Ye shall defend your families even unto bloodshed. Therefore for this cause were the Nephites contending with the Lamanites, to defend themselves, and their families, and their lands, their country, and their rights, and their religion" (Alma 43:45–47).

Knowing this, I could serve willingly and with honor.

Another example: We once had a major decision to

A testimony

DOES NOT

burst upon us suddenly.

Rather it grows,

AS ALMA SAID,

from a seed of

FAITH.

make. When our prayers left us uncertain, I went to see Elder Harold B. Lee. He counseled us to proceed. Sensing that I was still very unsettled, he said, "The problem with you is you want to see the end from the beginning." Then he quoted this verse from the Book of Mormon, "Dispute not because ye see not, for ye receive no witness until after the trial of your faith" (Ether 12:6).

He added, "You must learn to walk a few steps ahead into the darkness, and then the light will turn on and go before you." That was a life-changing experience from one verse in the Book of Mormon.

Life moves all too fast. When you feel weak, discouraged, depressed, or afraid, open the Book of Mormon and read. Do not let too much time pass before reading a verse, a thought, or a chapter.

My experience has been that a testimony does not burst upon us suddenly. Rather it grows, as Alma said, from a seed of faith. "It will strengthen your faith: for ye will say I know that this is a good seed; for behold it sprouteth and beginneth to grow" (Alma 32:30). If you nourish it, it will grow; and if you do not nourish it, it will wither (see Alma 32:37–41).

Do not be disappointed if you have read and reread and yet have not received a powerful witness. You may be somewhat like the disciples spoken of in the Book of Mormon who were filled with the power of God in great glory "and they knew it not" (3 Nephi 9:20).

Do the best you can. Think of this verse: "See that all these things are done in wisdom and order; for it is not requisite that a man should run faster than he has strength. And again, it is expedient that he should be diligent, that thereby he might win the prize; therefore, all things must be done in order" (Mosiah 4:27).

The spiritual gifts described in the Book of Mormon are present in the Church today—promptings, impressions, revelations, dreams, visions, visitations, miracles. You can be sure that the Lord can, and at times does, manifest Himself with power and great glory. Miracles can occur.

Mormon said: "Has the day of miracles ceased?

"Or have angels ceased to appear unto the children of men? Or has he withheld the power of the Holy Ghost from them? Or will he, so long as time shall last, or the earth shall stand, or there shall be one man upon the face thereof to be saved?

"Behold I say unto you, Nay; for it is by faith that miracles are wrought" (Moroni 7:35–37).

Pray always—alone and with your family. Answers will come in many ways.

A few words or a phrase in a verse, such as "wickedness never was happiness" (Alma 41:10), will tell you of the reality of the evil one and how he works.

"For after this manner doth the devil work, for he persuadeth no man to do good, no, not one; neither do his angels; neither do they who subject themselves unto him" (Moroni 7:17).

Generations of the prophets taught the doctrines of the everlasting gospel to protect "the peaceable followers of Christ" (Moroni 7:3).

Mormon saw our day. He issued this warning: "Except the Lord doth chasten his people with many afflictions, yea, except he doth visit them with death and with terror, and with famine and with all manner of pestilence, they will not remember him" (Helaman 12:3).

The central purpose of the Book of Mormon is its testament of Jesus Christ. Of more than six thousand verses in the Book of Mormon, far more than half refer directly to Him.

The Book of Mormon is an endless treasure of wisdom and inspiration, of counsel and correction, "adapted to the capacity of the weak and the weakest [among us]" (D&C 89:3). At once, it is rich in nourishment for the most learned, if they will humble themselves (see 2 Nephi 9:28–29).

The Book of Mormon confirms the teachings of the Old Testament. It confirms the teachings of the New Testament. It restores "many plain and precious things" (1 Nephi 13:28) lost or taken from them (see also 1 Nephi 13:20–42; 14:23). It is in truth another testament of Jesus Christ.

Over the past years, much has been written and said to attempt to discredit Joseph Smith. There always were, are now, and ever will be those who stir into 200-year-old dust, hoping to find something Joseph is alleged to have said or done in order to demean him.

The revelations tell us of "those that shall lift up the heel against mine anointed, saith the Lord, and cry they have sinned when they have not sinned before me, saith the Lord, but have done that which was meet in mine eyes, and which I commanded them" (D&C 121:16). They face very stern penalties indeed.

We do not have to defend the Prophet Joseph Smith. The Book of Mormon: Another Testament of Jesus Christ will defend him for us. Those who reject Joseph Smith as a prophet and revelator are left to find some other explanation for the Book of Mormon.

And for the second powerful defense: the Doctrine and Covenants, and a third: the Pearl of Great Price. Published in combination, these scriptures form an unshakable testament that Jesus is the Christ and a witness that Joseph Smith is a prophet.

And I join the millions of others who have that testimony, and bear it to you in the name of Jesus Christ.

Index

List of Illustrations

All images are used by permission.